The American Theory of Church and State

LOREN P. BETH

Professor of Government
University of Massachusetts

UNIVERSITY OF FLORIDA PRESS
GAINESVILLE
1958

To Carol and the Girls

A UNIVERSITY OF FLORIDA PRESS BOOK
PUBLISHED WITH ASSISTANCE FROM
THE FORD FOUNDATION

COPYRIGHT, 1958, UNIVERSITY OF FLORIDA
Library of Congress Catalogue Card No. 58-13204

PRINTED BY RECORD PRESS, INC.
ST. AUGUSTINE, FLORIDA

Preface

ANY AUTHOR owes a debt of gratitude far wider than he can consciously see; even at the level of consciousness, acknowledgment could hardly be given to all who in some way shared in the creation of the work. Nevertheless a few people are so directly involved in the production of the present work that it becomes a pleasant duty to express my gratitude for their help.

Jerome G. Kerwin of the University of Chicago guided my original studies in this field and provided critical analyses of the early drafts. His benign encouragement to a young and inexperienced student is greatly appreciated. The work was also read in earlier forms by Milton Konvitz of Cornell University and Leo Pfeffer of the American Jewish Congress. Valuable comments as to form and substance were contributed by Harry Kantor and Manning J. Dauer of the University of Florida. And kindly encouragement of the effort of publication was given by many colleagues and friends. To all of these my appreciation is extended.

It is trite to conclude prefaces by remarking that one's colleagues are not responsible for the final product, but in a controversial work such as this one such a statement is of special importance. I am solely responsible for all interpretations and conclusions contained herein.

v

Table of Contents

Introduction

THE NUMBER of recent books and articles published on the subject of church and state is ample evidence that the American idea of separation has not settled all conflicts between these two ancient institutions. Questions of religious education occupy the forefront of attention. As a matter of fact, the content of this rush of publications seems to indicate that there exists in the United States, not only an interest in the subject, but a basic uncertainty as to what separation of church and state actually is and what it means for modern America.

This study is an attempt to go behind the controversy and accomplish two things: to find out what separation really is and to validate it in modern terms. This cannot be done merely by reading the Constitution of the United States and the opinions of the men who wrote it, relevant as such studies may be. No recent American writer has attempted to do for the modern United States what John Locke did for seventeenth-century England or what James Madison and Thomas Jefferson did for Revolutionary America. Almost without exception modern works have been inconclusive because their authors have failed to look far enough back in American history and because they have concentrated on legalisms rather than on political and social theory. In addition, much of the recent writing has been by

1

spokesmen for various religious groups, and they are implicitly or openly concerned with the welfare of their particular churches rather than with that of political society. This study frankly emphasizes the political implications of separation. Why was separation politically desirable in 1789? Is it politically wise today? And if so, why?

In order to base the resultant theory solidly on our American tradition, as well as on the social "facts of life," it has seemed necessary to investigate at some length the historical growth of religious toleration and of the theory and practice of separation. What have been the insights of the great Anglo-American political thinkers who helped to shape American political thought? What of the currents of religious and political thought? How may these affect modern problems?

The final part of the book constitutes an attempt to construct a political theory of separation which is relevant to the conditions of American life today and at the same time true to our traditions of freedom. The result is in no way definitive; however, my hope is that it will stimulate thought and discussion on a vital problem of our times.

It should perhaps be emphasized that I have not tried to be impartial —an attempt which in any case would have been a failure. Even the rapid reader will be aware that I believe in separation of church and state in a fairly extreme form. I have not attempted to disguise this belief. Instead I have followed the precept of a wise "elder statesman" in the field of political theory, who states it thus:

[A writer] can make no profession of impartiality beyond that fidelity to sources which is the obligation of every serious historian, or beyond that avowal of conscious preferences which should be expected of every honest man. In any other sense the claim of detachment is a superficiality or a pretense.*

*George H. Sabine, *A History of Political Theory* (New York, 1937), p. viii.

1

The English Background

UP TO THE TIME OF THE American Revolution, immigration into the American colonies was predominantly English. The immigrants brought their religious and political ideas with them from England, and a study of the theory of separation of church and state in America would be incomplete without some knowledge of the conditions existing in the England from which the colonists came. As long as the colonies remained tied to England, they could not but be affected by events in the home country. Then, too, their cultural fare was mostly provided by English books and pamphlets. It was of course inevitable that in the course of time English customs and theories would be given a distinctively American flavor, but this fact neither denies nor invalidates the statement that American thought was based on British thought, on the subject of church-state relations as on other topics.

For this reason it seems necessary to spend some time in the consideration of English developments during the colonial period. This consideration is prompted by the belief that American political thought can only be understood by reference to its English background.

During the colonial period, and indeed to the present day, English practice in church-state relations never got beyond the stage of toleration; in England church and state are still not separate in the

American sense; and thus the problems of the present day are somewhat different in the two countries. But this difference was not true of the seventeenth century, and then some English thinkers who had a powerful influence on American thought advocated complete separation.

1

When Jamestown was settled in 1606 the problem of religious toleration was just beginning to be significant in England. Although even after that date the Puritans, who were the major extremist group, were still encompassed within the official Anglican church, neither they nor the conservatives were particularly happy with the arrangement. After James I's accession in 1603 the question of the position of religious dissenters was a constantly vexing one, for the dissenting groups were neither static in size nor quiet.

The seventeenth century was still a time of great religious fervor. The educated men were mostly religious leaders, or at least they had been educated in religious or semireligious institutions. It was thus inevitable that the growing conflict have a largely religious tone because few of the thinkers could conceive their ideas in secular terms. Most of the thought was directed toward the welfare of the church rather than toward that of people or state. The main consideration was the salvation of man, not his freedom or his well-being on this planet. It was 1760 before a really secular thinker appeared, and even Hobbes often couched his arguments in religious terms.

It should be stressed that those who opposed toleration were neither bigots, dissemblers, nor fools, necessarily. Uniformity of religion was still a well-nigh universal ideal, and a chief cause of conflict was the impossibility of reaching the ideal. It was natural that believers in the ideal would, considering the fervor of seventeenth-century religion, use harsh methods in their attempts to achieve it.

Not only was religious opinion deemed to be within the legitimate sphere of state action, but uniformity at least in religious organization was thought to be a political necessity if the state was to be stable and secure. The established government was threatened twice by minority groups, first by the Roman Catholics and later by the Protestant dissenting groups. For their own security the Tudor and

Stuart monarchs regarded uniformity as a necessity, and their supporters naturally agreed.

Finally, in this period each religious group strongly believed that it embodied the whole of religious truth and that no other group could therefore possess any. Such a situation led almost necessarily to the belief that all other religious groups were schismatical and heretical and therefore not to be tolerated. Toleration was an impossibility so long as such beliefs were held.

Any substantial degree of toleration, then, had to await a time when social conditions permitted its growth. When religious diversity had reached a certain point, toleration became both a political and a philosophical necessity. Even then, however, public opinion was only partially ready to accept it. It remained for the accompanying growth of rationalism to destroy the belief in an exclusive church before toleration could be freely accepted in religious circles.

This prevailing belief in religious truth as enunciated only by one's own church was responsible also for an anomalous situation in which various religious groups could ask for toleration for themselves while they were in a minority, with no intention of granting it to other groups if they gained power. Only some Baptists and the Quakers, as groups, rose above this serious obstacle to real toleration.

The reign of James I (1603–1625) saw the gradual disintegration of a religious *modus vivendi* which had been precariously established by the popular and tactful Elizabeth. James was stubborn and opinionated, although not actually very intolerant. He had been unhappy under his Presbyterian tutors in Scotland, whose high pretensions seemed to him incompatible with absolute monarchy. The Scottish churchmen thought that the church should govern the state; that the king, in Melville's words, was merely "God's silly vassal" enthroned to put into effect the gospel according to Calvin and his heirs. James was thus, after he escaped from this rigid tutelage, not eager to grant much to the Puritans, who were the English compatriots of the Scottish religious leaders. He felt that a king was God's earthly vicar with no ecclesiastical intermediary, and he concluded that it was his duty to protect his absolute God-given religious leadership against ecclesiastical usurpation.

James was a firm believer in divine right and absolutism; he claimed the power to "legislate for the Church with the cooperation of Convocation only, without reference to Parliament,"[1]* a stand which ensured Parliamentary opposition. And to add to the difficulty, James felt it his Christian duty to use his power to maintain the "true" religion—Anglicanism—in his domain. As both a religious and a political measure, the prince must suppress dissent in his realm.

Nevertheless James was not temperamentally intolerant, and consequently there was little active persecution during his reign. What there was he usually placed at least nominally on political grounds. In a day when religious dissent was regarded as tantamount to political treason, this was not hard to do. It may almost be said that James's failure in religion was due to the fact that he was unwilling to persecute harshly enough to kill dissent, yet was too intolerant to pacify it; the major effect was to make the dissenters, and more especially the Puritans, "narrower and more militant."[2]

The position of the Puritans was a peculiar one. They had arisen long before James's time within the Anglican church, asking for a real reformation. Whereas the conservatives were satisfied with the Elizabethan settlement, which retained church doctrine, hierarchy, and ritual almost unchanged from "Popish" days, the Puritans leaned doctrinally more and more toward Calvinism, demanding wholesale "purifications" in dogma, ritual, and organization. Neither side was willing to compromise to begin with, and James's espousal of the conservative side made a split irrevocable, even though the Puritans did not finally break from the Church for many years.

Various small groups also existed during James's reign which had already given up any hope of reforming the Church of England from within. Most of these were Calvinist sects; the implications of their beliefs were tolerationist, since they stressed the idea of personal religious experience and judgment which theoretically, though not in practice, made doctrinal orthodoxy a minor matter. In practice they were anything but liberal in their attitudes toward other beliefs. They wanted toleration, but only for themselves, not for others. Their thought is important, then, not for its effect on their practice, but because it had tolerant implications far beyond what they could themselves have envisaged.

*Notes to this chapter begin on page 156.

There were, it is true, a few early Baptists who were Mennonite rather than Calvinist and who went far beyond most other groups in their belief in toleration; but they were too few to be very influential. In effect it was the very growth in both size and variety of dissenting groups, not their beliefs, which provided the most powerful argument for toleration.

2

Under Charles I the split within the Anglican church came into the open. Charles gave the intolerant William Laud the position of Archbishop of Canterbury. Laud proceeded to attempt a re-establishment of the ecclesiastical authority which had been largely unused by his immediate predecessors. He further antagonized the Puritan minority both in and out of Parliament by suppressive religious measures and by an apparently pro-Roman bent. In return for Charles's support, Laud was obligated to give ecclesiastical aid to the king. As a result of these conditions, by the early 1640's Parliamentary and Puritan opinion, both political and religious, was so inflamed that it engendered a willingness to take to arms in its defense. It was Laud's principles that caused the break in the Church of England, combined with the stubborn and fanatic insistence of the Puritans on a real "reformation."[3] For "the key to the Civil War is that the quarrel of the nation was not with Monarchy, but with Charles; not with the Church, but with Laud";[4] and the fact that monarchy and prelacy were mutually supporting aggravated the crisis in both church and state. This close alliance proved disastrous to the Church, but it was necessary to the Laudian party, which was a small minority. Conversely, Charles needed church support as a prop, not perhaps for monarchy, but for *his* monarchy. Absolute monarchy and absolute episcopacy went hand in hand, and the two together were the cause of the revolution which was ahead—a revolution which was to destroy Charles and his pretensions as well as the dominant position of the Church.

The Laudian regime was important to the growth of the American colonies because the opposition of two forms of stubborn intolerance —Laudian and Puritan—was one of the factors causing a large emigration of Puritans to the American colonies. Trevelyan calls Laud, with some exaggeration, "the founder of Anglo-Saxon supremacy in the New World."[5] Most of the émigrés were Calvinists and most of them went to New England, thus bringing Calvinism, with all its intolerant practices and all its tolerant and democratic implications, to dominance in that area. But in addition the emigration seriously depopulated some rural sections of England, depressing property values and leading some thinkers to conclude that intolerance did not pay in practical affairs.

Various individuals fought, unsuccessfully, the widening schism in Anglicanism. Even though their efforts proved fruitless, in attempting to provide for the encompassment of widely differing religious ideas within one church, they perforce had to investigate and enlarge the permissible boundaries of toleration. The ecclesiastical members of the group are called the "latitudinarians" because of their belief in allowing wide latitude of faith within the church. As a rule they believed that a man's faith can be determined only with the use of his own reason; that the fundamentals of Christianity are few, simple, and obvious; and that beyond these fundamentals there are no points of ritual or dogma important enough to justify intolerance.[6]

These attitudes were shared to a large extent by a group of laymen, mostly politicians, called the "Erastians" after the Swiss divine Thomas Erastus. In some cases this group went almost to the point of open religious skepticism. Francis Bacon, for instance, found it hard to find *any* religious principle fundamental enough to justify intolerance! The Erastians may also be distinguished by a belief that the state should control religion—a control which, they held, would assure at once both unity and tolerance. They had a sneaking feeling that religious truth could not be demonstrated rationally, but only subjectively; religious men were incapable of achieving toleration, and Erastians were disposed to hand the job over to the state. The Erastians, then, were notable because they were the first of the *secular* thinkers; the good of the state they regarded as being of greater significance than that of the church, and thus they emphasized the common law and the necessity for governmental control of the church in order to assure internal peace and stability.[7]

Nevertheless, there were significant limitations to latitudinarian and

Erastian thought on toleration. It implicitly restricted toleration to Christians. The Erastians, hating fanaticism and fearing civil disorder, would have checked not only non-Christians, but all extremist or fanatical sects, presumably including such obvious examples as Baptists and Quakers, and even the Puritans themselves.[8]

The final solution of the religious problem in England was to be more Erastian than latitudinarian and more expedient than philosophical. But both groups of thinkers, by casting doubt on the infallibility of any system of religious truth and by emphasizing reason and moderation in a period of fanaticism and extremism, laid the groundwork for the future settlement.

3

The Puritan group had little to offer in the way of toleration in any direct sense. Puritans had no objection to persecution as such, and they believed in an intolerant state church to which all citizens must be forced to accede. They were not struggling for freedom but for supremacy within the Church of England. They hoped to erect a state church on the Scottish or Genevan model. James I with his Scottish upbringing was aware of this aim, and its incompatibility with his concept of monarchy was clear both to him and to Charles— a fact which largely explains their unwavering opposition to Puritanism. In addition, the Parliamentary opposition to the king's prerogative was closely tied to the Puritan opposition to the conservative prelates, for of necessity Puritanism was as closely tied to Parliament as the Anglo-Catholics were to the throne.

Yet there were two considerations that mitigated Puritan intolerance. First, Puritanism was a minority faith. When not in power it had to plead for toleration, even though it did not believe in it, and its arguments could easily be appropriated by others. When it *was* in power, Puritanism's minority status forced it to make concessions to other sectarian groups in order to preserve its own dominance. Secondly, in spite of its doctrine of the Elect, Puritanism had obvious implications leading toward toleration. These implications sprang from the Puritan emphasis on individual Bible-reading and individual religious experience and from the lack of efficacy, according to its own

9

theory, of persecution as a means toward salvation. The large number of sects springing from Calvinism testifies to the dynamic nature of this individualism; and the radical sects were to have far more influence toward freedom than the strict and conservative Puritans. It may therefore be well briefly to mention some of the other groups.[9]

The Independents were Puritans who, while wishing to remain within the Church of England, had given up hope of reforming it entire and asked only to be left alone within it.[10] The Separatists, again Puritan in religious belief, had left the Church of England in despair of a reformation but were willing to live alongside it as long as they were left undisturbed in their own worship. The Pilgrims who landed at Plymouth Rock belonged to this group.[11] The most liberal on the question of toleration were the Calvinistic Baptists, who held to toleration as a tenet of faith rather than as a mere expedient; their thought could easily embrace the idea of separation. Roger Williams was a Baptist when he formulated the theory of separation, as we shall see.[12]

4

The English Civil War was both a religious and political struggle, but for reasons we have already seen, the religious groups found it politically necessary to line up with either king or Parliament. The Anglo-Catholic element in the Church of England naturally supported the king, and so did the latitudinarians who feared Puritan fanaticism, the Erastians who stood for the maintenance of traditional political authority, and the Roman Catholics who had nowhere else to go. On the side of Parliament were found the Puritan sects and the other more radical religious groups. Thus there were conflicting groups within each coalition, with differing aims and policies. This was particularly true of the Parliamentary forces—a seventeenth-century "popular front" which was bound to fall prey to internal division as soon as the royalists were defeated. It was this split which kept the way open for the Restoration.

Cromwell, personally a tolerant individual, was prevented by this split and by the necessities of military rule from providing England with much toleration; but during the war and the Interregnum appeared the first substantial pleas for anything beyond comprehension within the church or toleration outside it. Therefore this period is of special importance to the development of the separation theory in America, particularly since at least two leading spokesmen for religious liberty, Roger Williams and James Harrington, had pronounced influence on American thought. The theories of the major writers of the period are thus worthy of somewhat more detailed consideration.

5

Roger Williams is one of the heroes in the American pantheon, and though he was English and wrote in England, his thought had much more influence in this country than in England. Williams stood far in advance of all but one or two seventeenth-century theorists, certainly ahead of both Milton and Locke, in his thought on church and state; and in some respects he was so far ahead of his time that we have not even today caught up with him.

Freedom of conscience was to Williams a natural right which was not given up to the state,[13] for each man was responsible for his own salvation which could be attained only through the exercise of his own free judgment.[14] "Without search and trial no man attains this faith and right persuasion," he wrote. This idea in itself was not particularly new, but Williams proceeded from it to advocate an almost complete dissociation of church and state. In effect he separated them into airtight compartments between which no conflict could occur. The church was to him a completely voluntary association which had no dependence whatever upon the state. He compared it to other associations of his day:

[The church is] like unto a body or college of physicians . . . like unto a corporation, society, or company of East India or Turkey merchants, or any other society or company in London; which companies may hold their courts, keep their records, hold disputations, and in matters concerning their society may dissent, divide, break into schisms and factions, sue and implead each other at law, yea, wholly break up and dissolve into pieces and nothing, and yet the peace of the city not be in the least measure impaired or disturbed; because the essence or being of the city, and so the well-being and peace thereof, is essentially distinct from these particular societies. . . . The city was before them, and stands absolute and entire when such a corporation or society is taken down.[15]

The church was to exercise no disciplinary authority beyond that of excommunication,[16] and it was to have no function beyond that of religion.[17] Masson, interestingly enough, expresses the view that Williams would not even permit the churches to have parochial schools.[18]

The functions of the state were to be similarly limited.[19] There could be no national church;[20] all religions must be tolerated. For, Williams held, the foundations of the state are the same whether it be Christian or heathen, and to grant the Christian state the right to foster Christianity would be to grant the heathen state the right to foster its false religion.[21] "All civil states . . . are essentially civil, and therefore not judges, governors, or defenders of the spiritual, or Christian state and worship."[22] He even implied, as a logical consequence of this reasoning, that the schools could not be permitted to teach any religion at all, thinking obviously of public schools.[23] And there were to be no civil disqualifications from the franchise, the right to hold office or to own property, on account of religious beliefs, because, as he put it, "if a commonweal be lawful amongst men that have not heard of God or Christ, certainly their officers, ministers, and governors must be lawful also."[24]

The radicalism of these proposals is easily seen when we consider that even today Britain has a state church, that the United States has parochial schools, and that under certain circumstances religion can still be taught in the American public schools. Three hundred years have not seen the full fruition of Williams's theories.[25]

Williams added compelling arguments that toleration and separation would add to the strength and stability, not only of churches,[26] but of the state. Economic progress would be stimulated and thus separation would be of positive material benefit to society.[27]

The magistrate, said Williams, if he were of any religion owed three things to that religion: approbation, personal submission, and protection; he owed two things to all other religious groups: permission and protection.[28] The supreme test of the seventeenth-century liberal was his attitude toward non-Christians. This test Williams

12

passed with colors flying, for he would bar none from toleration or from the rights of citizenship; he would accord liberty of belief even to Turks, Jews, and pagans.[29]

In sum, as Wolfe remarks, "Williams was one of the first reformers to sense the impossibility of Protestants ever again achieving unanimity of opinion even in a broad sense."[30] He thus gave up the ideal of comprehension which had animated so many great minds from "the judicious Hooker" to "the ever-memorable" Hales and turned to separation as the only answer. Was such extreme separation a real possibility? Certainly not in Williams's day, perhaps never.[31]

6

In the advancement of the principle of general freedom of thought John Milton has rightly been given a major place; *Areopagitica* is one of the classics of human freedom. On the more restricted problem of freedom of the religious conscience, however, he was not as far-sighted nor as broad-minded. He was not as radical as Williams or Henry Vane, nor as statesmanlike as Cromwell, nor as charitable as the latitudinarians. The question of how highly to rate Milton's contribution is difficult to answer in view of its lack of influence both in England and in America. It is probable that the Milton "cult" has tended to overrate his importance.[32]

Like Roger Williams, Milton typifies the "leftward" drift of English religious thought during the seventeenth century. Both men began as good Anglicans, became Puritans, and progressed from this position to differing degrees of unorthodox religious thought. Williams became a Baptist, but after a few years he found even this advanced position too confining. He lost connection with any group and carried on instead as a "Seeker," believing in the constant search for new revelations of the divine will. Milton became an Independent, but he too, by the end of his life, could be connected only tenuously with any organized group.

Milton's thought was shaped by two dominant and partially con-tradictory influences: Puritanism and rationalism. These influences are typical of the period; in Milton they were mixed into a curious blend which produced both tolerance and intolerance. While he could and did attack persecution in religion with mighty rhetoric, he also damned the intolerance of the Laudian party with all the intolerance of which the Puritan was capable, and he never reconciled himself to the toleration of Catholicism or of non-Christian faiths.

The early part of Milton's career, as far as toleration and religious freedom are concerned, was conspicuously barren. He accepted whole-heartedly the Puritan conviction that the word of God set down an exact form of government and that all human and ecclesiastical government must be renounced if it should be in conflict with this *jus divinum*. He would accept no compromise and denounced those who, like the latitudinarians, proposed it. He attacked episcopacy and supported presbytery with all the vigor of which his talented pen was capable. He failed then to see that Puritan rigidity would be as persecutory as was that of Anglicanism.

By 1645, however, Milton had awakened to the fact—experienced earlier, and personally, by Williams in Massachusetts—that presbytery was no better than episcopacy, and in *Areopagitica* he began his attack on "the new forcers of conscience." Giving up the idea that Scripture provided an obvious guide to government, he was convinced instead that truth could be attained only through progressive search carried on by the free reason of man, with the guidance of Scripture. "When God gave [Adam] reason, he gave him freedom to choose, for reason is but choosing," he wrote.[33] We do not have all truth, nor shall we ever have it until the second coming; we should there-fore not forbid nor hinder the continuing search for it.[34] He welcomed freedom as the test of truth; "who ever knew truth put to the worse, in a free and open encounter?"[35] and saw that in such an encounter diversity of belief was necessary and desirable. "If all cannot be of one mind, as who looks they should be? this doubtless is more wholesome, more prudent, and more Christian, that many be tolerated rather than all compelled."[36]

But *Areopagitica* was principally a plea for a free press,[37] not for religious liberty which it touches upon only incidentally. And Milton's Puritanism forced him to restrict liberty to (at most) only Protestants. He continued: "I mean not tolerated popery, and open superstition, which as it extirpates all religious and civil supremacies, so itself should be extirpate, provided first that all charitable and compassionate means be used to win and regain the weak and the misled."[38]

Milton, in *Areopagitica* and later, never argued for a full freedom, for he drew a sharp distinction between liberty and *Christian* liberty. "One is the liberty which all men equally may claim under the secondary law of nature. . . . The other is the liberty which all men would have possessed had Adam remained upright but which is now to be claimed by good men and believers."[39]

Milton had by 1659 advanced to the advocacy of separation. Religion, he said, is "our belief and our practice depending on God only . . . there can be no place left then for the magistrate or his force in the settlement of religion, by appointing either that we shall believe in divine things, or practice in religious."[40] This position, however, was largely vitiated by Milton's restriction of religious liberty to "true" Christians. In his definition this group included all who base their belief on the Scriptures alone—thus all Protestants.[41] But those who hold "opinions not probable by scripture"[42] are heretics, because error is merely a matter of misunderstanding while heresy is a belief held by the will and choice.[43] Catholics are therefore heretics, and even if they could be tolerated on political grounds (which Milton did not grant), they could not on religious; Catholicism if public "gives grievous and unsufferable scandal . . . to all conscientious beholders," and if private gives "great offence to God."[44]

Milton had inveighed against "these fantastic terrors of sect and schism";[45] but he fell prey to the same fears himself, and his fears destroyed his tolerance. For how can church and state be separated if the state has the duty of suppressing any religious group? Intellectually Milton all but destroyed the grounds for religious persecution, for the individual stands alone with his reason with no aids to find the truth; yet Milton was never able to break through his Puritan preconceptions to the sort of freedom that Williams and William Penn attained. His mind "was still dominated by the need for defending acknowledged truth in religion"; therefore he could admit only *Christian* liberty in *indifferent* things.[46] Liberty was for him a sadly restricted concept; it was, as Barker says, a Gospel privilege belonging only to true Christians (as Milton defined them), not to all men.[47] Milton did not seem to be really interested in religious liberty, or at least he was not aware of its full implications. His concern was with "true religion, not religion, with the Christian magistrate, not the magistrate, and with Christian liberty, not liberty."[48]

7

The thought of Thomas Hobbes presents in more than one way an antithesis to that of Milton. While Milton wrote advocating toleration but with intolerant reservations, Hobbes wrote in defense of absolutism, but his thought had implications leading to toleration. Again, Milton wrote for freedom and republic, while Hobbes wanted dictatorship and monarchy. Still again, Milton was religious and concerned, perhaps primarily, with the salvation of man, but Hobbes was completely secular and concerned with peace and order in this world.

To Thomas Hobbes, who wrote *Leviathan*—"a very wicked book, with a very strange title"[49]—the experience of the English Civil War proved one thing: that peace and order are the conditions most to be desired in this world. All his political writings are devoted to the defense of a system of government that will obtain this end.[50] The maintenance of order demands an absolute sovereign to whom all rights except that to life are given up.[51] The absolutism of the ruler extends to religious belief as well as to civil affairs, for although no laws can bind the conscience ("no man . . . knoweth the heart or conscience of a man, unless it break out into action. . . ."[52]), they can and must control the actions to which conscience may lead. Hobbes goes into an elaborate and finely spun proof that obedience to the sovereign is not incompatible with obedience to God or to conscience. "Such obedience, even contrary to conscience, is not sin; because since he has given up his judgement to the government, the command is his as well as that of the government, so that he is still obeying his own conscience in a sense."[53]

Thus the sovereign has complete control of religious belief and practice. Eternal good is better than temporal good; hence the ruler ought to establish the religion in which he himself believes.[54] He is to have "the sovereign power, to be judge, or constitute all judges of opinions and doctrines, as a thing necessary to peace;"[55] he shall by right decide "what doctrines shall be held and professed concerning the nature of God and his operations."[56] It "pertains to *temporal right* to define what is *spiritual* and what *temporal.* . . ."[57]

Furthermore, Hobbes maintained that national unity in religion is essential, that in fact the church and the state are two heads of the same coin. Temporal rulers derive their authority from God, and that authority extends to the church as well as to political affairs.[58]

Temporal and *spiritual* government, are but two words brought into the world to make men see double, and mistake their lawful sovereign. . . . There is . . . no other government in this life, neither of state, nor religion, but temporal; nor teaching of any doctrine, lawful to any subject, which the governor both of the state, and of the religion forbiddeth to be taught.[59]

And again:

A city of Christian men and a Church is altogether the same thing, of the same men, termed by two names, for two causes. For the *matter of a city* and a *Church* is one, to wit, the same Christian men. And the *form*, which consists in a lawful power of assembling them, is the same too; for it is manifest that every subject is obliged to come thither, whither he is summoned by his *city*. Now that which is called a *city*, as it is made up of *men*, the same, as it consists of *Christians*, is styled a *Church*.[60]

Church authorities thus have no coercive (or any other) power but what is granted them by the sovereign.[61]

Within this setting of absolute power the actual extent of toleration is left by Hobbes largely to the sovereign judgment. He would prefer, however, that the power be exercised in a tolerant manner. He asks "that there be no prohibition without necessity of any thing to any man, which was lawful to him in the law of nature"; that is, "that there be no restraint of natural liberty, but what is necessary for the good of the commonwealth."[62]

Religion for Hobbes had in effect "no other foundation than the law of the land," as Burnet says.[63] In fact, Hobbes had little religious feeling and little belief in religion. Religion springs from fear of the future and of the unknown forces of the present; it is merely superstition played upon by cunning priests who desire to gain power and control society.

And in these four things, opinion of ghosts, ignorance of second causes, devotion towards what men fear, and taking of things casual for prognostics, consisteth the natural seed of religion; . . . these seeds have received culture from two sorts of men. One sort have been they, that have nourished, and ordered them, according to their own invention. The other have done it, by God's commandment, and direction: but both sorts have done it, with a purpose to make those men that relied on them, the more apt to obedience, laws, peace, charity, and civil society.[64]

The state stepped in to control and exploit this powerful force, "to make it believed, that the same things were displeasing to the gods, which were forbidden by the laws."[65]

Jordan calls the Hobbesian tolerance "the tolerance of spiritual death," and in a real sense this description is true.[66] Hobbes practically destroys religion as a thing which can be believed; the tolerance he advocates is a tolerance proceeding from indifference rather than from charity. It is here that the major part of the Hobbesian influence for toleration lies, in that his skepticism, like that of Bacon, was symptomatic of a growing indifference to religion throughout society. When religion is unimportant, persecution is unnecessary. Religious beliefs which are at the mercy of a ruler's caprice are not beliefs for which men will persecute or die. We arrive at the view that "all religions are of equal value, because none are of any," except for political purposes.[67]

Hobbes's thought also led to toleration by reaction. It is only natural that in a day when religion was still the dominant motive, the Hobbesian doctrine should be rejected; we have seen that Burnet, a liberal churchman, regarded it as evil. As a matter of fact, it was the most sensational and oft-refuted doctrine of the century. In the reaction to Hobbesian absolutism it was inevitable that "the separability of what Hobbes had striven indissolubly to unite" (church and state) would be realized.[68] In this realization lay an acceptance of liberty of conscience.

8

James Harrington is a somewhat neglected figure today in America, which is all the more strange since he enjoyed a great vogue among

Revolutionary leaders such as James Otis, John Adams, and Thomas Jefferson. His "authority was freely quoted in the discussions which preceded and followed the elaboration of the American Constitution. His works formed the political bible of Otis and John Adams, and Jefferson's copy is . . . in the library of Congress."[69]

In the field of religious liberty Harrington was not a pioneer nor a great synthesizer. He was neither as radical as Williams, nor as brilliant as Milton, nor as relentlessly logical as Hobbes. His importance seems to lie, rather, in the fact that his very moderation was more representative of the mass of English opinion than were the more striking qualities of these contemporaries. In some respects, moreover, he was more discerning than they. He was a moderate liberal, shrinking from extremes either of right or of left.

The contribution of Harrington for his own day, and perhaps also for ours, lay in two rather striking additions to the theory of religious toleration. He was the first English thinker to see any connection between liberty and forms of government. First, he believed that religious liberty and civil liberty are Siamese twins, neither of which can live alone. "Without Liberty of Conscience, Civil Liberty cannot be perfect; and without Civil Liberty, Liberty of Conscience cannot be perfect."[70] Of the thinkers we have so far studied, only Milton approached this concept, and in Milton it is largely implicit, perhaps unconscious. Second, and perhaps more important, Harrington felt that civil liberty (including liberty of conscience) is incompatible with monarchy and is fully attainable only in a republic. Peculiarly enough, here again Milton arrived at much the same conclusions at about the same time, though again not as explicitly. It should be noted that Harrington used the word "democracy" as we would today use "republic."

Democracy being nothing but intire Liberty . . . must admit of Liberty of Conscience. . . . Absolute Monarchy pretends to Infallibility in matters of Religion, imploys not any that is not of its own Faith, and punishes its Apostats by death without mercy. . . . Democracy pretends not to Infallibility, but is in matters of Religion no more than a seeker, not taking away from its People their Liberty of Conscience.[71]

Harrington thus arrived at that connection of civil liberties with representative government which has been one of the chief characteristics of liberal democratic thought ever since.

Harrington's fear of extremes prevented him from including Catholics, Jews, and idolaters in the permitted freedom of worship; he did not, however, say that their beliefs should not be tolerated. Within this limit there was to be no bar to public worship nor to the holding of public office. The grounds of the exclusion are not convincing,[72] and fit in poorly with his belief that no religious group is infallible.

[The Commonwealth] pretends not to Infallibility, but comes . . . to raise up her hands for further light. . . .[73] [The Commonwealth] shall suffer no coercive Power in the matter of Religion to be exercis'd in this Nation. . . . Nor shall any gather'd Congregation be molested or interrupted in their way of worship (being neither Jewish nor Idolatrous) but vigilantly and vigorously protected and defended in the Injoyment, Practice, and Profession of the same. . . .[74] Liberty of Conscience intire, or in the whole, is where a man according to the dictats of his own Conscience may have the free exercise of his Religion, without impediment to his Preferment or Imployment in the State.[75]

Harrington believed in a national church on grounds reminiscent of Hobbes, but much less uncompromising, for he would make the national church purely voluntary, with no coercive power whatever. There must be a national religion because

a Commonwealth is nothing else but the National Conscience. And if the conviction of a mans privat Conscience produces his privat Religion, the conviction of the national Conscience must produce a national Religion. . . .[76] [Nevertheless] such as are of gather'd Congregations, or from time to time shall join with any of them are . . . left to the liberty of their own Consciences, and to the way of Worship which they shall chuse, being not Papish, Jewish, or Idolatrous.[77]

In Harrington's ideal commonwealth as delineated in his *Oceana* the care of religion is vested in a national Council of Religion which is to be elected annually by the Senate. It is to judge and arbitrate in the national religion and to protect liberty of conscience.[78]

We see at work in Harrington's thought much the same influences

20

that were noted in that of Hobbes: rationalism coupled with an almost complete secularism. Both men are interested mainly in the political effects of religion and in how these effects can be so tempered as to be no longer dangerous to the peace and order of political society. The results, however, are much different in Harrington's moderation than in Hobbes's fright. It is significant in judging the importance of Harrington to note that the Toleration Act of 1689 accords in its main outline with his proposals: a state church without coercive power and with provision for freedom of Protestant dissent. It is also a vindication of his theories that this solution came only with the revolution of 1688 which produced a constitutional monarchy approaching the republicanism Harrington thought necessary to the existence of liberty of conscience.[79]

9

One more figure of the Interregnum deserves some consideration. Henry Vane was a Parliamentary political leader and a Puritan who migrated to Massachusetts Bay Colony and became its governor; he returned to England because of his disagreement with colonial leaders over their handling of the affair of Anne Hutchinson. Vane used his influence in Parliament in an attempt to secure an Erastian solution to the problem of church and state, believing that religious affairs should be dominated by Parliament. Not an extremist, he also advocated the establishment of some limitations on the power of the legislature.

During the Hutchinson controversy in Massachusetts Vane argued that he as a magistrate had a duty not to base his rule on hostility to any religious opinions. It was a supreme law, he declared,

that all magistrates are to fear and forbear meddling with giving rule or imposing in these matters. They are to content themselves with what is plain in their commission, as ordained of God to be his minister unto men for good, while they approve themselves the doers of that which is good in the sight of men, and whereof earthly and worldly judicatures are capable to make a clear and perfect judgment: in which case the magistrate is to be for praise and protection to them.

But the magistrate may not exceed the civil jurisdiction; to do so is good neither for the state nor for the people, and fosters civil disorder. Religious freedom Vane bases on divine and natural law— those things "that God hath exempted" from the magistrate's commission.

Vane went on to propose that this restriction of state power be laid down in a written constitution, a solution which Harrington proposed at about the same time and which the short-lived Instrument of Government had contained a few years earlier. Vane opposed the Cromwellian regime on the ground that government must be based on popular consent and that a freely elected parliament observing the popular will is the true safeguard of religious liberty.[80] Vane was therefore one of the first to develop the idea of popular consent and of a limited constitutional government based on a written constitution. This idea was echoed by Locke and the framers of the American Constitution, and it can be considered a direct forerunner of the First Amendment to that Constitution, if not the pattern for it.

10

After Cromwell's death the Presbyterian faction gained a shaky dominance in England, and in the hopes of consolidating its position this faction eventually joined the Anglicans in inviting Charles II to return to England. Thus ended the Interregnum.

Although on the surface the problem of toleration was left in the same position as before the Civil War, the flood of tolerationist literature had produced its effect: the theory of toleration was, by 1660, complete. Henceforth, however persecution or intolerance might be practiced, it could not be justified except on grounds of expedience and revenge.[81]

Religious control after the Restoration was largely retained by Parliament, which led to the strange spectacle of kings asking for a toleration in which they did not believe merely in order to assert their authority against that of Parliament; yet when Parliament passed a Toleration Bill in 1681 it was rejected by the king!

The key to this anomalous situation seems to lie in the fact that neither Parliament nor king was really interested in toleration, but each party was much interested in political power. The Stuarts wished to regain the royal prerogative in all its Tudor splendor; Parliament wished to maintain its own political supremacy. The religious question was for each party a means, not an end. It is evident that Charles II had no interest in toleration; while he was not himself a religious man, he felt that such an authoritarian monarchy as he desired could not safely grant much religious liberty. "He said often," writes Burnet, "he thought government was a much safer and easier thing where the authority was believed infallible, and the faith and submission of the people was implicite."[82] For political purposes, in order to retain the friendship of the Catholic French king, he was impelled to make some gestures toward toleration; but he knew well the political value of an established church firmly tied to the throne, and he never let these gestures mean very much.

Parliament for its part was too much afraid of the king, of a return to Catholicism, and of a new Civil War, to be willing to offer much in the way of toleration; and most of the persecution of the Restoration period was sponsored by Parliament for these political purposes, rather than by the church for religious reasons. In other words, religious intolerance was practiced by the political authorities for political reasons. Such repression, however, was likely to be short-lived, since it was based on fear and a desire for revenge; the fear would die down as the war receded into history, and the desire for revenge would disappear with it.

Parliament still acted on the idea—no longer practicable—that religious uniformity was both desirable and possible. Between 1660 and 1672 acts were therefore passed which ejected all dissenting clergymen from their posts in the Anglican church on the basis of a test oath; forbade dissenters from serving as municipal officials or in the national civil, military, or Parliamentary service; made dissenters' meetings illegal; and prevented dissenting clergymen from even approaching towns in which they had once preached.[83] While these laws were rigid and harsh, Charles enforced them only half-heartedly in order to spite Parliament.

As the Catholic designs of Charles, and later James II, began to be apparent, Parliament began to forget its fear of dissent in order to solidify all possible political support against the king. Eventually monarch and assembly found themselves engaged in "excited competition" for the favor of the dissenting groups.[84] James issued a Declaration of Indulgence in 1687—with the joker attached that acceptance of it would imply the acceptance also of a royal prerogative even beyond that of the Tudors. The Church of England at this point deserted the throne and allowed Parliament to pass its own Toleration Act (1689), after James had been forced to abdicate and flee the country. Thus toleration came to England as a part of a politico-religious struggle to prevent the return of Catholicism and of royal absolutism.

The only spokesmen for toleration during the Restoration period who were significant for American thought were William Penn and John Locke, the first because of his attempts in Pennsylvania to put theory into practice, the second because of his great influence on American revolutionary thought.

William Penn was the greatest nonconformist writer during the Restoration. Yet it was probably his high connections at court and his opportunity to test his theories in the New World rather than the significance of his ideas in themselves that made him an important figure. Penn used largely the same arguments as Williams and Milton had used earlier, but with greater stress on the economic gains to the state that would supposedly result from toleration. He opposed religious tests as qualifications for office. Like Williams he had a belief in toleration that was not merely negative; it was held on a priori grounds, for the Quaker belief in the doctrine of the inner light left no room for outward compulsion. It is not, said Penn, reasonably within the "Reach of Humane Power to fetter Conscience."[85]

Penn argued his case particularly with a view to the rising propertied and merchant classes.[86] From a political point of view, however, probably his strongest argument was the claim that men should not be deprived of public office because of their religion. He based this idea not only on their rights as individuals, but even more perhaps on the loss to the state when capable public servants must be refused employment.

Prejudicing Men in their Persons or Estates, or depriving them of any Station in the Government, they might otherwise, in their Turn, be capable to serve the Publick in, is contrary to the Tenderness and Equity [of Christianity].[87]

Is it not an odd thing, that by leaving them on foot, every Body shall have Liberty of Conscience but the Government? For while a man is out of office, he is Test-free, but the Hour he is chosen to any Station . . . he must wiredraw his Conscience to hold it, or be excluded . . . can this be equal or wise? Is this the Way to employ men for the good of the Publick, where Opinion prevails above Virtue, and Abilities are submitted to the Humour of a Party . . . ?[88]

In the laws which accompanied the *Frame of Government* of Pennsylvania, Penn's principles of religious liberty were put into effect. It was provided that all

who confess and acknowledge the One Almighty and Eternal God, to be the Creator, Upholder, and Ruler of the World, and that hold themselves obliged in Conscience to live peaceably and justly in Civil Society, shall in no wayes be molested or prejudiced for their Religions Perswasion or Practice in matters of Faith and Worship, nor shall they be compelled at any time to frequent or maintain any Religious Worship, Place or Ministry whatever.[89]

In spite of its obvious limitations this was for 1682 a broad grant of freedom, equalled perhaps nowhere in the world except in Roger Williams's Rhode Island colony or Henry Robinson's charter for the Bahamas. Thus principles which could be held but not practiced in the Old World were put into practice in the New.

11

It may be valuable at this point to summarize briefly the forces which impelled in 1689 a toleration which had proved unacceptable to all sides only thirty years earlier. In addition to the political situation which we have already surveyed, the mental climate in England had changed drastically.

The theory of toleration, as we have seen, was substantially complete by 1660. The pioneer work had been done by such men as Williams, Milton, and Harrington. Under Cromwell, indeed, some limited toleration had been put into practice, but the Anglicans gave it up when they were returned to power with the Restoration.

Two principal things seemed necessary before a general acceptance of toleration was possible: first, a realization that a unified national religion was no longer possible, so that attempts at repression were futile and led to sedition and disorder rather than to security; second, a conviction that toleration would be a positive boon to the country, that it would encourage trade and commerce and restore internal peace and good feeling. It will be noted at once that these are practical and expediential, not theoretical, considerations. In short, the practical man of affairs with political influence—the merchant, the shipper, the Parliamentary leader—had to be convinced of the necessity and practicability of toleration. This is perhaps the reason why great theorists did not arise during the Restoration; even Penn's most telling arguments were those directed at the men of business and of politics.

The religious fanaticism of the Civil War and Interregnum could not be maintained indefinitely. It was bound to wear itself out, and the process was aided by the ideas of the great theorists which slowly percolated through the religiously and politically conscious sections of the populace. People gradually became readier to accept differences of opinion as inevitable if not beneficial.

Perhaps more important than the writings of any specific controversialist, however, were various social influences which were at work throughout Europe in the seventeenth century. The Protestant Reformation led inevitably to an individualization of religion and thus eventually to a religious attitude that would accept toleration. At the same time the growth of rationalism and of the spirit of science destroyed much of the trust the educated man could put in the infallibility of any particular religious theory. Coupled with this change in the *spirit* of belief there was an actual decline in the *strength* of belief. The new science, the spread of trade and commerce, new geographical discoveries, and new colonies occupied men's minds to the partial exclusion of religion, and sometimes led to outright skepticism or unbelief. The present world had become for most men more important than the next. Religion was no longer the center of life; it needed to be identified no longer with politics. Rather it had become only one interest among many. On its religious side this change was marked by the tolerant spirit of such men as

Penn or Bishop Burnet, and on the political side by the rise of the Whig party which for the first time put politics on a nontheological basis.

Not only were Whig leaders laymen, but many of them were not religiously inclined; or at least religion was to them a peripheral interest. Their thought had been shaped under the new influences—rationalism, science, a growing utilitarian spirit—which led to the conviction that society is based on a social compact; that men do not and cannot give up certain natural rights; that the state is concerned with men's bodies, not their souls; and that the state is limited in its proper sphere of action. When Roger Williams based liberty of conscience on the inalienable rights of man, when William Penn attacked the penal laws because they interfered with the rights of property, or when Sir William Temple pointed to Holland's prosperity as being a result of her toleration—these arguments struck a responsive chord in Whig minds. The theory of toleration held that uniformity of religious doctrine is not politically essential; that the Christian state may not promote any particular kind of Christianity; and that men may worship as they please as long as they do not interfere with public order. Such principles the Whig lords like Shaftesbury and Halifax consistently supported; to them they added the "three things the ideal Whig must love": law, liberty, and the constitution—and an instinct for the protection of property and commerce.[90]

Yet in spite of the great intellectual changes which made it possible, the Toleration Act itself was proof that the old ideas were still strong. For the act to modern eyes seems noteworthy more for what it did not do than for what it did. It did not abrogate the penal laws; it merely exempted certain groups from their operation. It did not grant the right of liberty of conscience; it merely granted toleration as a grudgingly given privilege. It did not even provide a complete toleration; it merely enacted a partial toleration of moderate dissenting Protestants. The state church remained, and the state power remained. For toleration does not imply that the state possesses limited rights; it means only that the state has decided not to exercise its rights, reserving of course its privilege of doing so in the future. Toleration is a concept of expedience, liberty is a concept of rights.

But if the toleration was not liberal, it was at least practical; and if it was merely expedient, it was admirably so. Indeed a good case can be made for the argument that it was the most that could be obtained at that time and in those circumstances. Toleration of Catholics was out of the question; even the toleration granted was greeted with no enthusiasm by the general public. And if full freedom was not given, at least "henceforth a man might be a citizen of England without being a member of the English Church."[91] The content of the act was determined by political considerations, and after all a political persecution can be countered only by a political toleration. In addition, its very conservatism was the best guarantee of its permanence. Even such an apparently innocuous piece of legislation as this one was to face the threat of annihilation.

12

John Locke's thought on the toleration problem was neither original nor radical; practically its every point had, as Laski pointed out, "been anticipated by one or other of a hundred controversialists."[92] And the force of his arguments as an influence for toleration was lessened by the fact that they were published in England only after the Toleration Act had become law, even though they had taken shape on paper as early as 1666. Locke's function was to synthesize the thought which had come before and to stabilize the solution that had been reached. Much as his political works served as a justification for the constitutional political settlement of 1688, so did his toleration letters justify the religious settlement of 1689. He made orthodox and respectable a theory which had already gained wide currency.

It does not seem necessary to comment at great length on Locke's tolerationist writings. The first letter is well known and has been much commented upon, and it contains all the important points in his theory. As has been remarked, it advances nothing particularly new; but it provides a soberly reasoned argument that would appeal to the businessmen and landowners which the dominant Whigs were.

Locke's thought was apparently "set" as early as 1666 when he wrote an essay on toleration which, however, went unpublished.

It was somewhat more conservative than his later thought, but otherwise it furnished a rather complete pattern for his first letter which was not published in England until 1689.

The most interesting and perhaps least known of Locke's works is the *Fundamental Constitutions of Carolina* (1669). His patron Lord Shaftesbury was, like Locke himself, one of the proprietors of the colony of Carolina; presumably Locke had much influence in the writing of the document. The *Constitutions* is a queer, almost medieval document in many ways. Its religious provisions require that all freemen shall acknowledge a God; that the Church of England shall be established; that dissenting churches shall be permitted, but only within the following regulations: registration of terms of admittance and communion and registration of membership. The terms of admittance must include belief in a God and must require that he be publicly worshipped. No one is to be protected by the laws or to be eligible for public office who is not a church member. Further, it is provided that no religious assemblies may be molested; that no one may speak "irreverently or seditiously of the government, or governors, or state matters"; that churches may not refuse membership to those accepting their terms; that persons may be excommunicated or may voluntarily leave their churches; that no abusive language may be used against any church; that churches not observing these rules are not churches, but may be punished as riots; and that no person shall be molested on account of his "speculative opinions" in religion.[93]

Even the brief paraphrase here given will make it obvious that this document is much more detailed and much more limited than Williams's Rhode Island charter or Penn's *Frame of Government*. It is probable that the provisions were shaped by other hands in addition to those of Locke; nevertheless all through his writings runs a strain of conservatism which prevents him from reaching the free ground occupied by Williams and Penn. Even in his letters on toleration Locke never included Catholics or atheists in the toleration he advocated. Implicit in all his thought is the idea that though no church should be established, Protestant Christianity should. This idea he shared with Milton, though for different reasons. For Milton included only "true Christians," with the argument that only they were deserving of liberty; while Locke drew the same limitations because he felt that other groups were menaces to human and political society.[94] On this essentially secular basis Locke concluded that although the care of souls was not the state's business, only Protestantism was safe for the state.

Here we can see clearly the great problem involved in the theory of separation of church and state—a problem which Locke side-stepped and of which his predecessors did not even seem to be aware. Admitting that lines must practically be drawn between the proper spheres of the religious and the political, how are these spheres to be defined and by whom? Locke tries to ignore the problem, merely remarking that if the state does not overstep its bounds, nor does the church, conflicts will rarely if ever occur.[95] He apparently believed that his formula was an absolute rule good at all times and in all places.

At the same time, however, Locke obscures the issue by saying that religious beliefs and practices are not to be tolerated if they are contrary "to those moral rules which are necessary to the preservation of civil society."[96] He never goes on to discuss the question of how these moral rules are to be determined, assuming presumably that they are obvious to everyone. Further, he seemingly had no conception of the possibility that social change may force changes in some of the moral rules; he seems on the contrary to have assumed without discussion that the rules are fixed and immutable. In no other way could he have avoided the question of who is going to decide what these rules are at any particular time.

With our increased knowledge of the processes of social change, we cannot follow Locke in ignoring the question. Consequently a good deal of the value of Locke's thought, and that of his contemporaries, is lost for present-day American purposes. Insofar as Locke faced the issue at all, he seemed to imply that the state would of necessity have to be the arbiter when conflicts arose (with the right of revolution reserved),[97] for he wrote from a political viewpoint which argued not only for separation but for the supremacy of the political. This is in essence the answer at which we have arrived in the United States. Its adequacy will be discussed in future pages.[98]

13

The passage of the Toleration Act did not ensure either the achievement of full toleration or the retention of that which had been accomplished. The majority of the Church of England divines were still opposed to *any* toleration, and in this they were supported by the powerful Tory faction in Parliament. These two groups sought outright repeal of the act, or at least its emasculation.

Fortunately William and Mary were sincere advocates of toleration. By a judicious policy of appointing to high church posts only latitudinarians like Burnet and Tillotson, they made sure that the church's intolerant majority could not control its policy. Politically they found it at length possible to appoint only Whigs to the cabinet. Thus for the twenty years of the joint reign the cause of toleration was kept safe, though it endured continuous assault. The policies of the government were such that neither Catholics nor non-Trinitarians were seriously repressed. There seemed to be no genuine enthusiasm for rigorous persecution, and toleration was now the status quo with all the strength such a position implies.

But if the policies of William and Mary entrenched the dissenters in their newly won privileges, those of Anne did not. The Whig downfall, brought about partly because of the Queen's animosity, was the signal for renewed attacks on nonconformity. The laws excluding dissenters and Catholics from civil offices were strictly enforced, and several new acts of repression were passed.[99] Only the death of Anne and the importation of George I from Germany prevented a frontal attack on the Toleration Act itself.

After the accession of George I, however, toleration was beyond effective attack, and even those discriminatory laws which remained on the books went largely unenforced. There was, in fact, during much of the eighteenth century little interest in theological questions even among the clergy. This indifference led, perhaps, to neglect and moral laxity, but at the same time it allowed sectarian jealousies to abate and so laid the foundation for the further expansions of the toleration policy which were to come later.

There is little of interest in political speculation after Locke. All the great thinkers, such as Hume and Berkeley, implicitly or explicitly supported toleration; but there was no advance in theory. It seemed as though eighteenth-century writers may have felt that Locke had said all that could be said on the subject.

Thus in 1776 when the American colonies broke away from the mother country, the problem of church and state had reached substantially its present status in England. There was a state church, more or less latitudinarian in concept, with toleration for dissent. In the main, church and state occupy the same position in England today.

The American colonists had thus imbibed by 1775 all that England could give in the way of a theory and practice of church-state relationships. Indeed, a few far-sighted Englishmen had brought to the New World concepts beyond those which had proved acceptable in the Old—concepts which were put to actual test in the colonies. The American theory of church and state, the development of which we shall now proceed to examine, is thus distinctively American, even though its origins lie in England. The men who developed the theory were English, but they had to come to America to try it out. The new and undeveloped continent offered a fertile field for experiment which the conservative constitutionalism of England could not provide.

2

Church and State in the American
Colonies, 1606-1775

IF THE THEORY OF TOLERATION attained fruition in England, that of separation, as we have seen, never did. The fact that separation is an American achievement has led many historians to assume that the colonists threw off the yoke of English religio-political ideas the moment they reached the new continent. A familiar version of the Pilgrim story depicts them as pioneers intellectually as well as spiritually, as coming to America to escape intolerance and to achieve religious liberty. This picture does not adequately portray the facts of the Pilgrim and Puritan settlements. As I have implied earlier and shall indicate further on, colonial America contributed practically nothing to the *theory* of religious toleration, much less to that of religious freedom. That definite contributions to the *practice* of these concepts were made is a fact both striking and true. But the fact is clear that colonial theories of church-state relationships were not indigenous to the American soil; they did not spring full blown upon the American strand; they were brought here by Englishmen, and throughout the colonial period they had their counterparts in English thought.

This fact should not surprise us, even though at first glance it may look like filial heresy. Ideas do not grow out of a vacuum, but out of a continuum. The English background of the colonists and their continued close contacts with England assured that their thought would be predominantly English for many years. Therefore it is natural and unremarkable to find that church-state relations in the colonies showed the same trends as in the mother country and drew their sustenance therefrom. We shall find, for instance, that the theory of a Congregational polity was not developed in America but in England and on the Continent; that the growth of toleration was as slow here as in England (and in some cases slower); and that as late as 1775 the American picture was not strikingly different from that of England.

Likewise the amount of difference between the colonies themselves has sometimes been exaggerated. Most of the colonists were English yeomen of fairly similar background; whatever their faith and whatever the colony to which they went, they carried with them the English idea of liberty and the English middle-class morality of the period. The Sunday laws of all the colonies, for instance, show that ideas of religious observance were similar whether the colony was Puritan, Quaker, or Anglican. The growth of strong dissenting movements and the Great Awakening also were influential in all the colonies.

However, such similarities between the colonies and the mother country, and between colony and colony, do not obscure the differences between them. After all, it was only in Massachusetts that Quakers and witches were hanged, and only in Rhode Island that formal separation of church and state was attained. There were as many gradations between these extremes as there were colonies, and on each colony English theory, practice, and political policy impinged to a differing degree. For this reason it is difficult to carry the argument of similarities to the extent either of considering the colonies as a whole or of including them with a discussion of English history. They require treatment separate from each other and from England.

In four colonies, perhaps five, for one reason or another the problem of church and state stands out in bold relief. These four deserve extended treatment in view of their importance in the struggle for religious liberty. They are Massachusetts, Rhode Island,

Maryland, and Virginia. The fifth, Pennsylvania, arrived late on the scene, and while both progressive and important, it did not play as decisive a role as did the others.

1

The researches of Perry Miller have pretty well exploded the old idea that the Congregational polity of the Massachusetts Bay Colony was derived from Plymouth after the Bay settlement was begun.[1*] That this idea could not be true should have been seen even earlier, since the Puritans, unlike the Pilgrims, always maintained that they had not separated from the Church of England. But even such recognition would not have answered the question of the actual source of the Congregational theory. It is this question that Miller has attacked.

Actually, except in ecclesiastical organization there was little in Congregational theory that was essentially different from the English Presbyterian variety of Puritanism which we have examined above. The theory was first of all an ethical-religious body of thought, and as such universal in its scope; but it was additionally, in a progressively narrower field of application, Christian, medieval, Protestant, Calvinistic, congregational-presbyterian, and theocratic.

Yet the differences between Presbyterian and Congregational thought, so slight that in Connecticut the Congregationalists eventually adopted Presbyterianism, explain to some degree the success of the Puritans in imposing their polity on the Bay Colony. Congregational thought believed that the true church could not be universal, but could include only those elected in the Calvinistic predestinarian sense. Each congregation was also, in theory, an independent unit of God's children, and no central hierarchical control was believed to be permissible or necessary; after all, if as Calvinists believed, God's rules as set down in the Bible were self-evident, complete unanimity would prevail even without such control.

Such beliefs sound necessarily separatist, for how could an exclusive and congregational church be a state church? Yet the Congregational thinkers never took the additional step of separation; on the contrary, they believed in a state-enforced uniformity of belief which they were perfectly willing, if circumstances permitted, to impose upon others. This obvious dichotomy left them open to attack from the Separatist side, but they clung to their attachment to the Church of England regardless. As Miller remarks, the Congregational thinkers— Henry Jacob, William Bradshaw, Paul Baynes, and William Ames— felt themselves compelled by the prevailing ideas of the early seventeenth century "to reconcile their Congregational dissent with the inviolable preservation of the principle of uniformity."[2] Consequently they stayed in the Anglican church, ever hoping that there would come a time when their beliefs would triumph; and in the meantime they claimed that as long as the Anglican church would keep them, it had the elements of a true church. As Ames, their greatest thinker, maintained, from a fundamentally true church "in which some wicked men are tollerated, we must not presently separate."[3] Good Christians came to service voluntarily, even though the general populace was forced to do so; and the godly members of a congregation accepted their nonelected ministers voluntarily (thus constituting his "call"), even though he was assigned to their church by the hierarchy. Such tortured construction of their doctrines left them always free to protest their loyalty to church and crown.

Those who never questioned that they should be coerced into conformity, even when a temporarily misguided monarch was coercing them in the wrong direction, might reasonably be considered loyal Englishmen.[4]

In hopes of some day attaining supremacy in England, then, Congregationalists could not resist the civil power over religion; on the contrary, they were forced to espouse it themselves. For instance, Ames wrote:

If therefore Heretikes be manifestly knowne and publikely hurtfull, they are to be restrained of the Magistrate by publike power. And if they be manifestly blasphemous, and pertenacious, and stubborne in those blasphemies, may suffer capitall punishment.[5]

Thus we find that the New England Puritan brand of thought as it developed in England inconsistently combined exclusiveness with uniformity and independent congregationalism with a state church imposed upon all. In matters of dogma, however, Congregationalism

36

is hard to separate from English Independency or from Presbyterianism.

The foregoing analysis of the thought of early Congregationalism explains much about the subsequent development of the "New England Way." But it leaves out one important point. If these men were willing, if not content, to remain in the English church, what was the reason for the migration to the New World? The old belief that they came because they were persecuted in England is now seen to be almost completely false. If, as Brooks Adams says, Hampden and Cromwell "could live and be returned to Parliament" under the Laudian regime, so could Winthrop; and there is no evidence that they were severely persecuted.[6]

Why then should these men leave home where many of them were people of some position and take a perilous voyage of thousands of miles to a largely unknown and unfriendly land populated by hostile savages? Some historians of the economic-determinism school maintain that they came largely to better their economic positions.[7] It is argued that the enclosure movement and the economic depression of the time hit especially hard the eastern counties of England from which most of the emigration derived. But enough was known of New England by that time (1629) to make it extremely doubtful to them that their economic status would be much, if at all, improved. It seems apparent that the economic motive, while undoubtedly present, was distinctly subsidiary to some other objective. We have not far to look for such an objective, once we have examined the Congregational doctrines outlined above.

As we have seen, Puritan thought required a reformation; and the more extreme the variety of Puritan, the more unwilling was he to wait for this reformation in dogma, ritual, and ethics. Thus the Congregationalists, who relied upon the conversion of the politically powerful for the success of their ideas, saw year after year go by without the king making any overtures to them or giving any sign that he was coming over to their point of view. Ultimately a break with the Church was inevitable unless the ruler was converted, since the Congregational polity demanded the support of the state. It was obvious to them that the longer they waited, the more they would be pushed into Separatism, an eventuality which they wished by all means to avoid.

Puritans could not arbitrate their cause. It was not that they refused to accept a higher judgment than their own; they honestly believed that their own judgment had not entered into the matter at all. They were only repeating the highest judgment ever recorded, and why the King would not listen to it was more than they ever could comprehend.[8]

The opening of the New World for English colonization presented itself fortuitously as the solution for all their problems. The only way to preserve the essential obedience to magisterial authority without betraying their beliefs was, obviously, to make sure the magistrates shared those beliefs. This could not be done in England, perhaps, but in New England, far from the Laudian arm, it could. If they could not make the Anglican church Congregational in England, they could do so in America.

Here we see very clearly why many Congregationalists turned to emigration as a solution. They could not wait for reformation of the English church; neither could they secede from it. But by leaving England and by accepting only believers to their new home, they could establish their Bible Commonwealth without being forced either to wait or to secede.

Because those who emigrated would come from the section of Puritanism which had never separated, they could call any church they established part of the Church of England, and therefore, by grace of magistrates of their own creating, could enforce complete obedience to it. They could . . . figuratively but effectively, transport both the English State and Church to Massachusetts and there reform them at will. Massachusetts would be a piece of England such as all England ought to be.[9]

It is clear, then, that the Puritan migration had a definite object and plan before it left England; it did not borrow this plan from Plymouth nor did it improvise after its arrival. This analysis explains why it was so important to the leaders of the movement to have a free hand once they arrived in New England—so important that contrary to all English colonial practice and with the aid of much extralegal hocus-pocus, they transferred the seat of the corporation from London where crown and church could keep close watch to America where corporation affairs could be comparatively safe from prying eyes. The Puritans came to America to set up their own kind of church, and necessarily their own kind of state, where the godly could live free from the contamination of the ungodly. This fact is the root of New England intolerance.

The religious homogeneity of the population, the transfer of the charter, and the early isolation from a troubled England resulted in the fact that in New England, not old, Puritanism reached its fullest flower and underwent its most severe test. The Congregational Way was completely dominant for many years, so that we can ascertain accurately what Puritanism really meant for the cause of religious toleration and liberty. The answer is that Puritanism was proved basically intolerant by the New England experience.

Puritanism rested upon a literal acceptance of the revealed word of God—the Bible—as the rule of conduct in both civil and religious life. Original Congregational theory held that congregations of believers formed and maintained independently of each other would yet agree completely because Biblical truth was obvious and self-evident to all who read and believed it. Therefore, it was at first thought that coercion of fellow believers would be unnecessary, whatever treatment might be needed for unbelievers. Congregationalism never explicitly rejected this belief, but in practice it soon became necessary to do so. For the Bible, like the American Constitution, is all things to all men; and if, as Byington uncritically writes,

Every man of them felt it was his right and duty to judge for himself in respect to all matters of truth and duty. It is an error to suppose that the Puritans were content to take their opinions from their ministers, or that the ministers themselves were agreed in respect to all points of faith or practice . . . ,[10]

the necessary result would have been spiritual and, considering the Puritan theory, political anarchy. The facts clearly contradict Byington. When laymen arrived at conclusions differing from the official line, as did Mrs. Hutchinson, Samuel Gorton, Vane, and the dissenters, they were not tolerated, nor were ministers like Williams and Wheelwright who differed markedly from their fellows. This was naturally and necessarily so. The Puritans came to Massachusetts to set up their own system, a system which included an intrinsic union of church and state. Such a system can stand criticism of neither the church nor the state. It rests upon a unitarian and authoritarian concept of life which must be accepted by all within its sway if it is to survive.

For the success of the Puritan Commonwealth, therefore, it early became necessary for the rulers of New England to evade two of the basic tenets of Congregationalism: the independent congregation and the free judgment of the individual. Thus there grew up an informal but effective church hierarchy, the "consociation" or synod, and an equally informal but even more effective union of ecclesiastical and civil authorities. In fact, it seems probable that the union of church and state in Massachusetts gained a good deal of its strength from its informal character; thus was John Cotton, for instance, enabled to deny that there was such a union, in his controversy with Roger Williams. It is also this informality which has posed a problem for later historians as to whether the colony was a political oligarchy or a theocracy. This discussion is sterile because the union of church and state was not based on the supremacy of one or the other, and the actual position of each in a crisis was debatable. It was based rather on an identity of viewpoint. Minister and magistrate were alike Puritan and church member. They thought and felt alike on most questions, so that in the day-to-day affairs of the colony the body of ministers and the governor and his assistants were almost always in agreement. There was no question therefore of supremacy except on a theoretical plane. The governor was the faithful member of the minister's congregation; the minister was the loyal subject of the governor's administration. And both alike were guided in all their actions by the Bible.

The Congregationalists consistently, and doubtless sincerely, looked to the Bible for guidance, and particularly to the Hebraic Old Testament:

Their God was the God of the Old Testament, their laws were the laws of the Old Testament, their guides to conduct were the characters of the Old Testament.[11]

[The Puritan] applied biblical phraseology to the affairs of life in a way that would have been impossible had he possessed any sense of humor.[12]

They believed that they had the means of knowing the mind and will of the Supreme Being . . . for the rule . . . of a community of human beings in a social, civilized state; that this Divine will was communicated by revelation, transmitted through a Book. Those who accepted this rule put themselves under a covenant of obedience to it, and this secured to them the right and privilege, and held them to the obligation, of compelling at least a respectful regard for it from all who were under their government.[13]

This literal belief could, on occasion, be carried to fantastic lengths, as Winthrop's history shows.[14] However, it is obvious from our viewpoint that uniformity of belief does not follow automatically from the reading of the Bible, and the Puritans were forced to conform their practice to this fact. Eventually not only was a systematized body of belief necessary, but also an ecclesiastical hierarchy which had the support of the civil authorities. The success of the salvation pilgrimage depended on the correct belief. And the correct beliefs, regardless of theory, were not determined by the individual Bible-reader, even as a member of an independent congregation; they were determined by the clergy. God's Word, indeed, was beyond question, but it needed interpretation and declaration, and the trained and learned clergy provided them.[15] Even the clergy, however, were not independent, for the synod was developed solely to bring clerical beliefs into accord, a duty which it performed admirably for many years. If in spite of social and religious pressure defection continued, it was the duty of the state to step in and enforce compliance.

The Scriptures were the rule of daily life; the ministers were the interpreters of Scripture. It follows that the ministers, aided and abetted by the cooperative state, had the power to enforce "the most far-reaching tyranny to which men could be forced to submit. . . . The cut of clothes, the names he bore, the most ordinary social usages, could all be regulated in accordance with the will of God."[16] The divine nature of the command made it no less tyrannical, especially to him who doubted its divinity! The sincerity of most of the New England leaders cannot be questioned, but neither can that of Laud nor that of James I. On such grounds "liberty cannot mean one thing in old England and another in New, nor can intolerance be condoned in the one and condemned in the other."[17] It does not really help the New England case to argue that the leaders were subject to the same rules as the general populace; in a system in which the leaders *make* the rules, subjection to the rules for them amounts to liberty.

The institutions of the new colony were built to embody these theories and practices. The towns were really church congregations; the town meeting, since only church members could hold the franchise and the meeting hall was also the church edifice, could convert itself into the church society at a moment's notice. The General Court, the governor and his assistants, and the body of the clergy (which was often called in to advise the political body) constituted a single oligarchy which ruled with complete authority over both church and state.

Under such circumstances it is certainly erroneous to maintain, as some historians have done, that the doctrines of Williams and the Hutchinsonians caused mere tempests in a teapot and did not really constitute a threat to the society. I have already stated my belief that an internal threat in any society is grave or minor according to the structure of the society. We cannot, therefore, say that Williams's doctrine of separation was not dangerous in Massachusetts just because we believe it to be harmless today. It is not dangerous today specifically because we now *have* separation; but it *was* dangerous to any society in which union of church and state prevailed. This constitutes perhaps the gravest charge against such union, for the intolerance which many consider to be the worst blot on New England's escutcheon followed from it. In a closely knit church-state "no civil question could be considered aside from its possible religious bearings; no religious opinion could be discussed apart from its political implications. It was a system which could be maintained permanently only by the most rigid denial of political free speech and religious toleration."[18] Only in such a political organization could such an obscure theological controversy as that involving Mrs. Hutchinson be a real and immediate threat to the state.

Intolerance was a necessity if the union was to be preserved. It seems, therefore, that it is the church-state union that we should condemn rather than the intolerance and persecution which were a necessary consequence of it. Thus we see that intolerance in Massachusetts, as Mecklin has pointed out, was of an institutional, not a personal, character. It proceeded from the peculiar ideology of the Bible Commonwealth and the institutional framework which was set up to effectuate it.[19]

It appears from this that much of the controversy between the filial-piety historians and their opposition occupies false ground. The weakness or newness of the state and the prevailing character of the age, for instance, have often been pleaded as extenuation for Massachusetts intolerance, and as often denied. But it is obvious, when one considers the early history of Rhode Island, Maryland, or Pennsylvania, that mere size or newness is no bar to toleration and liberty; and an age which held these colonies, plus Holland, and produced men like Chillingworth, Williams, Robinson, and Cromwell, cannot be blamed for the defects of Massachusetts or of Winthrop, Cotton, or Endicott. It was, it is clear, not the weakness of the state but its theory and constitution which produced intolerance; it was the intolerance not of the age but of men bred in the Congregational theory which produced persecution. John Cotton and Nathaniel Ward were neither pleaders of circumstantial necessity nor spokesmen for their age; they were merely examples of the men that Congregational theory bred.

So far we have been concerned mainly with Congregationalism's attempts to deal with defections within its ranks. It was no more tolerant in its dealings with outsiders, nonbelievers. This should not surprise anyone familiar with Puritan thought in England. A Bible Commonwealth such as Massachusetts was intended to be had to be kept pure, forcibly if necessary. The founders of the colony never intended to admit persons who dissented from the religion of the state; it was apparent even before the Hutchinson controversy that to exclude them legal means must be added to vigilance.[20] While the nature of Puritan thought prevented the inclusion of all inhabitants as church members, those who could not qualify as members were nevertheless expected (under considerable legal and social pressure) to pay taxes for the support of the Congregational church, to attend its services, and strictly to refrain from forming or joining any dissenting congregation or voicing any forbidden opinions. Within these limitations those not church members, who at all times apparently made up a majority of the population, were free to believe as they pleased.

Provided a man conformed to all the regulations of the church, paid his taxes, and held his tongue, he would not, in ordinary circumstances, have been molested. . . . But the moment he refused implicit obedience, or, above all, if he withdrew from his congregation, he was shown no mercy.[21]

Intolerance of dissent was, then, inherent in Congregational theory. It was also a practical necessity if the Wilderness Zion was to succeed. The colony was begun as a place where godliness could be made the rule of life; if it was to remain such, no infractions of that rule could be allowed. Historical testimony is unanimous that none of the Puritans regarded Massachusetts as any place for the practice of religious liberty. On the contrary, they regarded toleration as one of the worst of vices, except in matters which they regarded as unessential (which, considering their fundamentalism, were few). The writings of Nathaniel Ward present a pungent example of this attitude:

First, such as have given or taken any unfriendly reports of us New-English, should doe well to recollect themselves. We have been reputed a Colluvies of wild Opinionists, swarmed into a remote wilderness to find elbowe-roome for our phanatick Doctrines and practises: I trust our diligence past, and constant sedulity against such persons and courses, will plead better things for us. I dare take upon me, to be the Herauld of New-England so farre, as to proclaime to the world, in the name of our Colony, that all Familists, Antinomians, Anabaptists, and other Enthusiasts, shall have free Liberty to keep away from us, and such will come to be gone as fast as they can, the sooner the better. Secondly, I dare averre, that God doth no where in his word tolerate Christian States, to give Tolerations to such adversaries of his Truth, if they have power in their hands to suppresse them.

He that is willing to tolerate any Religion, or discrepant way of Religion, besides his owne, unless it be in matters meerly indifferent, either doubts of his own, or is not sincere in it.

44

How all Religions should enjoy their liberty, Justice its due regularity, Civill cohabitation morall honesty, in one and the same Jurisdiction, is beyond the Artique of my comprehension.[22]

More sophisticated writers, such as Cotton, denied that the colony persecuted for cause of conscience, but they agreed that the welfare of the state depended upon the maintenance of unity in the true religion. Cotton—whose career is one of the best American examples of always winding up on the winning side[23]—believed that union of church and state, with church predominant, was the Biblical and therefore the only justifiable way of government. This position was based upon his belief that only the godly state could prosper—a derivation, as Parkes maintains, from the primitive idea that God must be propritiated to assure good harvests.[24] "It cannot be well," Cotton wrote, "with a Commonwealth that liveth in bodily health, and worldly wealth, but yet without Churches, without Christianity, without God."[25]

The Puritans believed they held the truth; certainly they held the power and had the strength of purpose needed to impose it and maintain it. Yet Cotton was a good enough casuist to deny that Congregationalists, in persecuting nonbelievers, assumed their own infallibility; for, he said, the church speaks with the voice of God, not of man. "There is a vast difference between men's inventions and God's institutions; we fled from men's invention, to which else we should have been compelled; we compell none to men's inventions."[26] Cotton went so far as to deny that compelling men to "God's institutions" was persecution. "If the worship be lawful in itself, the magistrate compelling him to come to it, compelleth him not to sin, but the sin is in his own will that needs to be compelled to a Christian duty."[27] Obedience to God could not be persecution, and therefore coercion used to compel men to obey God constituted obedience!

Thus, in the name of God and to maintain undefiled the godly community, Puritan persecuted Quaker, as before him Catholic had persecuted Protestant and Anglican had persecuted Puritan.

The formulation of the Cambridge Platform in 1648 was the culmination of the Puritan dominance. They could now without opposition "legislate against heresy and Sabbath-breaking, they could force attendance upon worship, they could control the press, they could make education serve the ends of religion."[28] This unquestioned supremacy, however, was to last for only a score of years. By the 1670's the Puritan oligarchy was on the downgrade, and the rising forces of dissent were to bring with them new regard for the rights of other men. Governor Leverett (1673) allowed the sects to meet in private undisturbed, and in 1678 the Baptists constructed in Boston the first dissenting church in the Bay Colony.

The gradual decline in Puritan power was brought about by a multiplicity of causes, chief among which were certain inherent characteristics of Puritanism itself. In the long run the Congregational discipline could not succeed. The static and negative qualities which New England Protestantism accentuated failed to fulfill all the needs of human nature, and Congregationalism failed to adapt itself to changing modes of thought and life which demanded a different religious emphasis. The struggle to maintain the exclusively church-member franchise and the stringent requirements for church membership were among the things that eventually led to a need for a different basis for the state's political structure. Thus a conservative Protestantism was sitting dangerously on the lid of an explosive mixture in which the old reforming, individualistic, dissenting tradition to Protestantism itself was a major ingredient. Congregationalism could not permanently stifle the splits within its ranks which these explosive forces brought about. Mrs. Hutchinson and Roger Williams could be banished, but the time came when liberalism within the church could not be got rid of so easily, unless the standing order was to be rent asunder—a consummation which actually developed during the Great Awakening and later when Unitarianism came to the fore.

Then too after the first generation of settlers was gone, there was a marked decline in the religious fervor which had upheld the Puritans in their trials and both sanctioned and caused their intolerance. The harsh and demanding code of Puritan behavior was not as attractive to the sons as to the fathers; they did not see its necessity, and it demanded more religiosity and inhibition than human nature could long endure once the first impelling enthusiasm had passed. The growth of trade and the consequent prosperity, which Puritanism encouraged, accentuated this trend. Finally, Puritan intolerance was eventually sure to fail in its purpose because repression produces only a forced obedience rather than a voluntary consent, and such obedience is bound to seek an end to its subjection. Thus the Puritan state from its very beginning was faced with a continual series of crises, each of which threatened to reduce the church-state to ruins, and each of which would have been dangerous only in a church-state. The apparent strength of Puritanism is revealed by these crises to have been only a constant fear which forced its leaders to harsh measures. In sociological terms, it may be said that a certain set of social conditions gave rise to a prevailing belief which was then institutionalized. Once institutionalization had taken place, the prevailing belief became static; it could maintain its dominance only by assuring that the social conditions which had given it birth remained unchanged. It had a vested interest in the preservation of that social system. But other characteristics of the belief itself, as well as outside events, forced social change. This left the institutions of the belief in an anachronistic position which made their eventual downfall inevitable.

The Puritans were, in a sense, isolationists. Massachusetts was their refuge from the contaminations of the world, and it was a place to be kept pure at all costs. But just as they failed in the long run to prevent the inner decay of their system, so they failed to prevent the growth of outside influences which impinged upon their dominion and threatened their security.

Perhaps the chief of these outside influences as a direct cause was the constant encroachment of other sects on Puritan territory. The Quaker persecutions caused a revulsion among even good Puritans; such actions seem to have done more harm than good to the Congregational cause. In any case, the struggle between a Puritan fanaticism backed by force and a Quaker fanaticism backed only by conviction resulted in utter defeat for the state church; and the Quaker victory was accompanied by victory for Baptist and Anglican. The Puritan stronghold had been breached, and the tide of dissent flowed through that breach ever stronger. The Great Awakening, in Massachusetts as in other areas, gave increased strength to the revivalistic sects, particularly the Baptists; and these latter held to their historical belief in separation of church and state, as did the Quakers. The awakening thus strengthened the forces of liberty at the same time that it weakened the standing order through dissension and division.

The policy of England, while it gave rise to the antagonism which was to end in revolution, also helped to bring about toleration. Anglican England could never accept a state church in any colony which was not Anglican, particularly when as in Massachusetts Anglican worship was prohibited. The long arm of British imperial policy required that the church follow the flag; and if the home authorities could not force an Anglican establishment on the Congregationalists, they could at least, by the revocation of the first charter and the tolerationist provisions of a new one (1691), force toleration of Anglican worship, which led naturally to toleration for other sects as well. They could also require that the franchise limitation to Congregationalist church members be lifted, a requirement which was long evaded by the colonial authorities, but which could not be avoided indefinitely.

Added to these forces opposing the Congregational establishment were the intangible influences of the new libertarian doctrines of the eighteenth century and the continued growth of rationalism in thought, which led to a progressive evolution on the part of many sincere and intelligent people first to latitudinarianism and then to deism, skepticism, and secularism. As we have indicated, such subtle influences on thought were not limited to New England; they came from Europe by way of England and, if anything, reached Massachusetts later than most places. But just as in England they had made uniformity in religion seem less important and persecution less defensible, so they did in New England; and once the belief in uniformity is gone, the way is cleared for the possible end of an established church. Finally, the example of more enlightened areas had an inevitable effect in Massachusetts. Religious liberty in Rhode Island did not, as was freely predicted, make civil government impossible; and the great tolerance prevailing in Maryland, Pennsylvania, New Jersey, and New York, while not in each case amounting to liberty, yet made Massachusetts seem medieval by comparison. Such influences are not measurable, but their importance is evident.

By 1775 the progressive relaxation of the hard hand of the

Puritan elder had reached a point where no sect could be banished, no belief forbidden. The shell of the established church remained, propped up mainly by a conservative propertied class which, not necessarily religious itself, regarded the church as a good influence and essential to the stability of the community. Religious taxes could still be imposed, although Baptists, Quakers, and Anglicans were exempted under certain conditions in a law which invited abuse by intolerant Congregationalist assessors. The church was still supported, in some cases financially, by the provincial government.

From this brief review of Congregational Massachusetts it becomes obvious that she was a follower, not a leader, in the struggle for religious freedom. This is so far true that she was the last American state to give up her ties with the church. Thus in America as in England the great contributions to religious liberty, in theory or practice, did not come from an established church or from the conservative wing of Calvinism. We must look elsewhere for the germination of the doctrine and practice of separation.

2

As late as 1775 Virginia was not a great distance ahead of Massachusetts in providing her citizens with religious freedom. To be sure, the Old Dominion did not go to the length of executing people for erroneous beliefs, but she was hardly hospitable to people who held them.

Even so, the climate of opinion in Virginia was much more conducive to freedom of conscience than was the repressive atmosphere of Congregationalism. The Anglican church in Virginia was neither strong enough nor fanatical enough, and religion in general was not vital enough, to make a consistent policy of intolerance possible. Religious policy was largely prudential; a new sect was persecuted only as long as its weakness made persecution politically feasible. This policy was partly due to the lack of a definite body of religious theory to which the political authorities were bound, beyond that of the maintenance of the Anglican establishment; and even in this the colonial government had an ambivalent position. For the strength of the establishment was largely based on the tie with England. Therefore to strengthen the colonial church meant to subject it increasingly to the English ecclesiastical hierarchy. This the colonials were unwilling to do, since what they wanted was an establishment under their own control. The result was that the Anglican church in the colony was too weak to fight off the encroachments of dissenting sects with much energy, whatever her desires may have been.

What actually occurred, then, was a policy of piecemeal toleration. Each sect was given toleration when it grew mature enough to be socially acceptable and large enough to be politically influential. For the Quakers this position (strangely) came early, legally in 1692 but actually somewhat earlier. With the acceptance by the dominion of the Toleration Act of 1689, which came in 1699, Presbyterianism came to be accepted except for its itinerant preachers, who were to be especially prominent during the Great Awakening in the 1740's. Full acceptance of the Baptists, who were regarded with much distaste by the solid citizenry and whose preachers were largely itinerants for many years, did not come until the Revolution. Because the persecution of Baptists in Virginia came so late, it has been called "the worst and most inexcusable assault on freedom of conscience and worship" in colonial history.[29]

The fact that the Virginia church was Anglican undoubtedly accounts for some of this backwardness, for Virginia never felt able to tolerate anything in advance of its toleration in England, and in most cases not until some time after. Dissent in general, however, had much the same status as in the mother country, and toleration was an accepted concept earlier than in Massachusetts, even though its practice often lagged. Also, the English-European background of the Virginia colonists made an established church seem not only inevitable but necessary, particularly in the absence of any theory to the contrary. Virginia had no Roger Williams, and the Baptists with their belief in separation did not attain great strength until late in the colonial period.

Yet, as indicated above, the establishment for various reasons never gained great strength. The reluctance to depend on the English hierarchy only partially explains this weakness. Another factor was the sparse settlement which, contrary to Massachusetts practice, was not concentrated in towns but scattered widely on comparatively large plantations. This made it hard for the ministers to give service adequately; parishes were too large for a central meeting place and congregations too small to pay very well. Such conditions failed to attract the able and conscientious ministers who were so prominent a feature of the New England churches. Consequently the quality of the clergy was low, sometimes descending to the licentious and the dissolute. The church came in many instances to retain little but a purely nominal allegiance from its members, and this lack of prestige was reflected by large defections to the sects.

The growth of the dissenting groups, especially the Presbyterian and Baptist, was intensely stimulated by the Great Awakening; people flocked from the nerveless Anglicanism to which they were accustomed to the new and vital revivalism of the itinerant preachers. The growth of dissent was by far the greatest single factor in the eventual downfall of the establishment, weakened as it was by its own incapacities.

In spite of the petty persecutions of the Baptists indulged in by the dominion just before the Revolution, the situation in Virginia far more than in Massachusetts held in 1775 the promise of a quick establishment of religious liberty. All that was needed was a push. The war provided that push, and Virginia became the first state after Rhode Island to make separation of church and state a principle of its being.

3

Maryland, like Massachusetts, has been the subject of some controversy over her part in the progress of religious liberty. It has been variously claimed that Lord Baltimore, the proprietor, was actuated in his tolerance by principle and by mere expedience. Likewise the colony has been credited as the first to grant full toleration since the Reformation, and conversely as having made "no special contribution to the cause of religious freedom."[30] In this welter of claim and confusing counterclaim authentic facts are hard to find.

What seems to be certain is that Maryland practiced religious toleration from her inception until 1689, except for an interval during the Puritan Revolution in the 1650's. Whether this toleration proceeded from a principle enshrined in Baltimore's heart or from his realization of the precarious Catholic position in Maryland is a moot point, and it makes little difference anyway. However, Maryland's toleration was of a very limited sort. It did not extend to atheists, Jews, or Unitarians, nor did it allow any speech disrespectful of the Virgin Mary nor any act inappropriate to Sunday as a day of worship. This is a limited toleration indeed; yet it was far advanced in 1649, and it proved to be a workable and practical arrangement which, had later generations permitted, might have been a good base upon which further liberty could be built.[31]

It seems also to be true that toleration in Maryland under the Catholic Lord Baltimore was strictly his own personal colonial policy based upon either his principles or his views of expedience. It was not the policy of the Catholic church, which under English law could have nothing to do with the colony. As far as any evidence to the contrary is concerned, however, the church may have approved Baltimore's course of action.

In 1689 the Protestants, who had been in the majority for many years (eleven-twelfths in 1675), gained complete and permanent control of the colony. The Church of England was established in 1692, supported by general taxation. The Anglican church was not much liked, and it was a distinctly minority communion, but apparently the prevailing Protestant dislike of Catholicism caused its acceptance. In 1704 the Catholics, who had first established toleration in the colony, were ungraciously forbidden to hold mass, to support Catholic priests or teachers, or to vote. As a consequence many Catholic families migrated to freer Philadelphia, where by 1775 they constituted the largest Catholic community in the colonies and enjoyed the right to worship publicly—one of the few places in the colonies where this was permitted.

This retrogression seriously detracts from any claim that Maryland might otherwise have as a leading influence in the fight for religious liberty. Nevertheless her pioneer work in the field had its effect and is justly a point of pride with residents of the state and with American Catholicism in general.

4

To Roger Williams and his "livelie experiment" at Providence goes the honor of being the first American government—and perhaps the first in the world—to establish complete separation of church and state and to enshrine in its fundamental law a full liberty of religious belief and practice. Since we have already considered Williams's beliefs in another connection, little needs to be said of the theoretical basis for this policy. Williams advanced the most radical proposal for religious liberty that the world had yet—or has yet—seen. As Parrington says, "the generation to which he belongs is not yet born."[32]

As far as America was concerned, the Rhode Island example was a convincing demonstration that civil government is possible without any connection with religion and without any pretense, even in theory, that uniformity of religious belief is necessary. This example, more than anything else perhaps, convinced other colonies and states of the workability and the desirability of separation. Many were the religious disputes in Rhode Island, but after the first few years they never threatened the stability of the government. And the mere fact of this continuing and stable colony "constituted an unanswerable argument against the correctness of the Puritan political philosophy."[33]

Separation was apparently fully developed in Williams's theory when he arrived at Providence, for he never made any attempt to establish any kind of state church, nor while he lived was there any church-state connection in education, so far as this writer has been able to ascertain. As early as 1647 this separateness of the spheres of religion and politics was formalized in a legislative enactment which prescribed that "all men may walk as their consciences persuade them, every one in the name of his God"[34] up to the point of transgression on the rights of society, which, as we have seen, Williams defined broadly as threats to civil peace.

This law was no mere pious promise. In 1657 the United Colonies—Massachusetts, Plymouth, Connecticut, and New Haven—fearing this breach in the wall of the church state in such close proximity, asked Rhode Island to follow their example in excluding Quakers. It should be borne in mind that at this time the Quakers were the most hated and feared sect in England and the colonies, a position to which their fanaticism perhaps gave them some title. Also, Williams himself bitterly opposed the Quaker doctrines and even went so far as to write a scurrilous pamphlet against them. Quakers were executed in Massachusetts and persecuted everywhere else in the English-speaking world. But Rhode Island was blazing a pioneer trail, not following an old one. She replied that the Quaker excesses were probably provoked mainly by the opposition to the sect, and that since she did not oppose them she felt no danger from them, and pointed out: "We have no law among us, whereby to punish any for only declaring by words, etc., theire minds and understanding concerning the things and ways of God, as to salvation and an eternal condition."[35] Further action in line with the principles of Williams came in 1658 when the first Hebrew congregation in English America was established at Newport.

When Williams finally decided to procure a charter, impelled by the machinations of Massachusetts, he induced Charles II to agree to the inclusion of a religious liberty clause. Since this charter was Rhode Island's constitution until 1842, Rhode Island was the first state of the future United States to have such a constitutional provision. The charter read as follows:

That all and everye person and persons may, from tyme to tyme, and at all tymes hereafter, freelye and fullye, have and enjoye his and their owne judgments and consciences, in matters of religious concernments . . . they behaving themselves peacablie and quietlie and not using their libertye to lycentiousnesse and profanenesse, nor to the civill injurye or outward disturbance of others.[36]

That in the same year Rhode Island should pass a law disfranchising Catholics (of whom there were then none in the colony) and non-Christians would not seem to conform with this charter. But it seemed for many years that she had done so. In the 1744 revision of the Rhode Island code such a restriction appeared, purporting to have been enacted in 1663. However, the colonial records do not give any such enactment. Recent research indicates that the law was interpolated, apparently sometime between 1688 and 1744 (probably in 1705) by an overzealous official or committee, and not acted upon legislatively. Moreover, it was officially expunged from the records in 1783.[37]

If we accept this view, the fact emerges that Rhode Island alone among the original states of the United States has never had any law which would limit the rights of members of any religious group. Her importance to our study of the development of the theory of separation lies in the fact that she successfully applied the theories of her founder; she was his laboratory, and she proved his experiment successful.

5

The other English colonies in America ranged themselves between illiberal Massachusetts and free Rhode Island in the matter of religious toleration and freedom. Detailed remarks about them seem unnecessary, since there was nothing remarkable about either practice or theory. By 1775 a large degree of practical toleration existed in all the colonies, despite what had been in some cases extreme conservatism in granting religious freedom to the people. The toleration had become particularly broad in the proprietary and royal colonies. However, this toleration was generally good only for Protestants. Nowhere except in Rhode Island were the Catholics free from political disabilities; but conditions had so changed since 1630 that "practically all of the colonies had reached the stage where the separation of church and state could be made legally complete."[38]

Although some of the forces which led in the direction of greater religious freedom have been discussed as they affected Massachusetts and Virginia, they were seldom purely local influences. They were partly the same as those which we have seen at work in England, and partly indigenous to America. They were all at work throughout the colonial period and in all the colonies.

Perhaps foremost among these forces was the prevailing weakness of the established churches; as we have seen in Massachusetts, even the strongest of the establishments had elements within it which forced it to accept toleration eventually as a necessity. We have also seen that in Virginia the Anglican establishment was handicapped by colonial conditions and lack of effective control from England.

The weaknesses of these two establishments are the more remarkable because in precisely these two colonies there was the greatest chance of success for them. The Massachusetts population was overwhelmingly Congregational in sympathy, even though the actual church membership was a minority, and Virginia was the only colony in which Anglicans predominated numerically.

In the other Congregational colonies—Connecticut and New Hampshire—the same weaknesses as in Massachusetts were apparent, and in general the state was less willing to use its force to protect the church from encroachments. But these establishments were strong and secure compared to those of the Anglican colonies. In no colony save Virginia were Anglicans in a majority; and if the English church was weak in Virginia, it was weaker still in North Carolina, Georgia, Maryland, and New York. The sole exception was South Carolina, where despite numerical weakness the Church was strong and well administered. The Anglican establishment reached its nadir in New York, where its adherents numbered only a small fraction of the population and the establishment was extremely tenuous despite the efforts of several royal governors, being practically restricted to four downstate counties. As the colonial period progressed, the Anglicans in all colonies suffered because of their tie with the increasingly unpopular English government.

The remaining colonies—Pennsylvania, New Jersey, and Delaware—had no establishments, although in Pennsylvania the Quakers dominated the government, despite increasing opposition, until the Revolution.

Both contributing to and caused by this weakness of the establishments was the amazing spread of dissent. There were various other factors involved in this growth of dissent than the loss of vitality of the state churches, however. Perhaps the chief of these other factors was the need of the colonies for increased population, which made them tend to accept people of any religious faith. Coupled with the conversions from Anglican ranks, this immigration meant that in almost every one of the colonies by the end of the colonial period the combined dissenting groups had a numerical advantage. In addition, the open frontier was a standing invitation to the persecuted both of Europe and of the colonies themselves; in order to hold immigrants within effective jurisdictional range it was necessary to treat them fairly well. In the colonies where toleration was an established policy early, as in New York, New Jersey, and Pennsylvania, the inflow of dissenters was so great that there was never any real possibility of an establishment. In other colonies the establishment remained weak partly due to the same factor. The tremendous boost given to the evangelistic sects by the Great Awakening was a distinct help in so strengthening them that they could fight effectively for equality.

A final factor increasing the bargaining power of dissent was geographical in nature. Throughout the colonies the established churches were strongest in the longest-settled areas; the frontier zones were hives of evangelical activity. But the necessity of protecting the colonies against Indian attacks, for most of the eighteenth century inspired by the French, made it necessary to placate the frontier groups which had to bear the brunt of these attacks. For all these reasons the dissenting churches grew stronger vis-à-vis the established churches; it was inevitable that eventually their pleas for equality should become demands backed by the political power of numbers.

We have seen that in Massachusetts official English opposition to Congregationalism was influential in forcing the grant of increased toleration after 1663; this was also true in Connecticut and New Hampshire. In several other colonies affirmative action by England had the same effect; the Crown's grant to Rhode Island of the 1663 charter is only one example of this policy of the home authorities, which was mostly restricted to those colonies in which the Anglican church was particularly weak. The Georgia charter of 1732 tolerated all Protestant groups. The same was true of New Jersey under the royal government and of New York under both the Dutch and the English. Under the Dutch, at least, this policy was largely prudential; when Stuyvesant began a persecution of Quakers in 1662, the Dutch West India Company which controlled the colony, doubtless with one eye on the tolerant Dutch government, intervened.

The consciences of men, at least, ought ever to remain free and unshackled. Let everyone be unmolested, as long as he is modest; as long as his conduct in a political sense is irreproachable; as long as he does not disturb others, or oppose the government. This maxim of moderation has always been the guide of the magistrates of this city [Amsterdam] and the consequence has been that, from every land, people have flocked to this asylum. Tread then in their steps, and, we doubt not, you will be blessed.[39]

In at least one case, however, the English authorities forced a less liberal policy to be enforced than already obtained. In Pennsylvania the home government forced the colony to enforce the Test Act which disfranchised Catholics, thus overruling Penn's earlier more liberal policy.

In the colonies south of Pennsylvania the authorities in London officially supported the Anglican establishments. But such support was often more nominal than real, and this fact resulted in a greater toleration than might otherwise have been the case. As Greene maintains, "British statesmen might favor the extension of the Anglican system, but they were rarely willing to sacrifice any material, political or economic interest for the purpose."[40] This fact shows up most clearly in the extreme hesitancy of England to appoint a resident Anglican bishop for the colonies, although this policy was no doubt also partly motivated by a desire to keep the control of the church in England.

The growth of trade and commerce which was especially prominent in New England and the middle colonies was a further important factor in inducing toleration; not only did it, by taking men away from home to lands practicing other religions, breed an indifference to sectarian differences, but it also made religion in general seem less important. Business and wealth tended to replace salvation as the main interest of men. This was encouraged by the Calvinistic tendency to regard worldly success as evidence of salvation.

Whatever the cause, it cannot be denied that religious indifference had by 1775 become a major influence in the struggle for tolerance and liberty. There is ample evidence that religious indifference in America reached its peak in the period from about 1765 to 1800; so pervasive was it that Sweet can write that the colonies contained "the largest proportion of unchurched in Christendom," and that many who were church members, especially upper-class members of established churches, were actually indifferent.[41] It is obvious that then as now the religiously indifferent are more tolerant than the fervent believers. There is no doubt that such attitudes powerfully aided those who actively strove for separation. Besides, even where indifference was not present, the same factors of rationalistic thought and the development of science tended to make religious belief more liberal and latitudinarian. Thus "natural religion," deism, and skepticism worked hand in hand with indifference to produce liberty. That the men who held such beliefs were as often as not leaders in the struggle for political freedom hurt the cause not at all; for if religious liberty could be connected with political, the triumph of the latter would assure the attainment of the former—which is exactly what was to happen.

We have already alluded to the growing strength of dissent as a major factor in leading to religious liberty. Perhaps of equal importance were the beliefs and policies of the dissenting groups. One of the strongest of the groups was the Baptists who, as we have seen, held separation of church and state as a religious principle enunciated in the Bible. These views were shared by the Quakers. Holding such tenets, the Baptists of Rhode Island and the Quakers of Pennsylvania were unable to use their political control to force or even to encourage any religious belief. They were aided and abetted in all the colonies by other sects (principally the Presbyterian) which, while not opposed to establishment per se, were forced to oppose establishment because they occupied a minority position.

Finally, it would be impossible to overlook the influence of the practical success of the separation principle as it evolved in Rhode Island and Pennsylvania. With such examples existing, it became increasingly difficult to claim, as Cotton had, that civil government can succeed only when it is in league with religion. Rhode Island was a far more effective answer to Cotton than the theoretical writings of its founder.

To summarize the progress of the American colonies toward religious liberty by 1775:

(1) One colony—Rhode Island—had complete separation of church and state.

(2) Three colonies—New Jersey, Pennsylvania, and Delaware—had no established church. But all colonies except Rhode Island had laws unfavorable to Catholics and non-Christians.

(3) Three colonies had Congregational church establishments—Massachusetts, Connecticut, and New Hampshire.
(4) Six colonies had legal Anglican establishments. In New York this really amounted to no establishment at all. The others were Maryland, Virginia, the Carolinas, and Georgia.

There was still a long way to go, but it was to be covered in a surprisingly short time.

3

Revolution and Constitution, 1775-1800

THE YEARS DURING AND FOLLOWING the Revolutionary War were to see the triumph in America of the principle of religious liberty. The theory of this principle, substantially complete as early as 1660, was now to be applied on a scale never before attempted. The practice of the widely accepted theory, however, was not to reach its complete objective in that era, nor in any since. Separation of church and state is incomplete today, even in the land which bore it.

1

The colony of Virginia—one of the most illiberal, as we have seen, of the thirteen—was to be the first to apply the Rhode Island principle and the most uncompromising in following out its implications. Conditions in Virginia had made the establishment ripe for a fall. Some of the factors—the weakness of the Anglican church and the growth of dissent—have been referred to previously. But there were others of perhaps equal importance. Chief among these was the rise in Virginia of a small group of political leaders, mostly men of some culture and leisure, who had devoted much time to the study of politics, law, and philosophy. Unlike members of the upper classes in some of the other colonies, these men were leaders in progressive thought, espousing early not only the revolutionary cause of freedom from England, but also the much more radical cause of democracy and individual liberty. The role of liberty-loving Virginians who distinguished themselves in early United States history is without parallel among the states. Among this group of leaders the influence of rationalistic thought reached its height in America. They were to a man latitudinarian, skeptical, or deistic in religion. They were religious in the liberal sense of not being tied to any creed or dogma, yet having profound religious convictions. But their inability to give allegiance to any religious sect was pronounced, and it led them to a conviction that religious liberty was both a necessity and a right. With such learned, liberty-loving, and influential leaders the cause of religious liberty could not help being coupled with that of political freedom both in the war with Britain and in the fight against political conservatism which was to follow.

The struggles for the separation of church and state began with the Virginia Constitutional Convention of 1776. They were, said Thomas Jefferson, "the severest contests in which I have ever been engaged," for "although the majority of our citizens were dissenters . . . a majority of the legislature were church men."[1]* Jefferson's party was only partially successful. Article XVI of the Declaration of Rights, while it substituted at James Madison's insistence religious liberty for mere toleration, did not rule out a state church, nor disestablish the existing one, nor deny the right of the state to control religious affairs, nor prohibit taxation for the aid of religion.[2] The article, drafted by George Mason, had the powerful support of Patrick Henry.

This lack of specific prohibitions on state action left Madison, Jefferson, and their followers unsatisfied. Consequently in 1779 Jefferson framed a bill for religious freedom. However, the legislature not only refused to pass this proposal but in the reaction after the Revolution actually threatened what had already been accomplished. Led by Henry who was apparently worried by the postwar decline in religion and morality, an attempt was made to enact a more liberal type of establishment which would provide not only for the Episcopal

* Notes to this chapter begin on page 161.

church but for all the dissenting groups as well. The means proposed to this end was a general tax for the support of all churches, an act which would effectually have established general Christianity as the state religion. Henry's bill was supported by Richard Henry Lee, George Washington,[3] and John Marshall, probably in the belief that Christianity was a necessity for the recovery and maintenance of both public and private morality.

Skillfully led by Madison, with the help of George Mason, George Nicholas, and John Taylor of Caroline (Jefferson was abroad), the opposition forced a postponement of the issue from the 1784 session to that of 1785. During the recess Madison penned his famous *Memorial and Remonstrance* which, widely circulated around the state, more than any other single thing swung the tide against the Henry proposal. Henry's accession to the governorship at this strategic moment deprived the legislative majority of his effective leadership. The general assessment bill, therefore, was defeated when it came to a vote. Pressing the advantage, Madison re-introduced the old Jefferson bill for religious liberty, and it passed in December, 1785. This bill forbade any kind of taxation for the support of religion and effectually ended any thought of a general or particular establishment in Virginia.[4]

What did these acts mean, and whence came the theories they expressed? An examination of the writings of Madison and Jefferson helps to provide an answer. However, it must be emphasized that in spite of the great influence of these leaders, passage of the separation bill could not have been obtained without substantial popular support. Such support came mainly from the two great dissenting sects, the Baptists and the Presbyterians. Presbyterians in England and Scotland had not been noted for their zeal for religious liberty, but in Virginia they were never established and were politically an underprivileged minority of the population. The first fact made them anxious to pull down the existing state church; the second made their own elevation to this position an impossibility.

It should not be assumed, however, that Presbyterian laymen were moved only by such expediential considerations. Many of them were sincere advocates of separation; one of the finest petitions for religious liberty was that sent to the Virginia legislature by the Hanover presbytery in 1776, which said in part: "there is no argument in favor of establishing the Christian religion but what may be pleaded with equal propriety for establishing the tenets of Mahomet."[5] Even so, Madison's testimony indicates that the Presbyterian position was an equivocal one. If the laity were impressed by the need for separation, the clergy were not, and at first they supported the Henry assessment proposal. Madison wrote that they "seem as ready to set up an establishment which is to take them in as they were to pull down that which left them out."[6] Later he recorded a change of heart "either compelled by the laity . . . or alarmed at the probability of further interference of the Legislature if they once begin to dictate in matters of Religion."[7] Madison hailed the switch with joy, especially when he reflected that it might also be impelled partially by Presbyterian jealousy of the Episcopal church, a feeling which had flared up again when the latter body was incorporated a year or so previously. His own view was that this action ended the threat of a coalition between them, which "could alone endanger our religious rights, and a tendency to such an event had been suspected."[8]

The Presbyterian change of heart was announced in a petition which opposed the assessment bill.

It establishes a precedent for further encroachments, by making the Legislature judges of religious truth. If the Assembly have a right to determine the preference between Christianity, and the other systems of religion that prevail in the world, they may also, at a convenient time, give a preference to some favoured sect among Christians: . . .[9]

This powerful Presbyterian support was added to that of the Baptists, who almost unanimously backed Madison. The Episcopal and conservative position was, in general, that religion was needed for the proper training of citizens and that therefore the state had a legitimate interest in the promotion of religion. The Baptists, on the other hand, denied such assumptions completely; they assumed that religion had nothing to do with the social order, that it was essentially a matter for the concern of the individual and his God— subjective, spiritual, supernatural. This position derived from that of Roger Williams, and it could only mean wholehearted support of the separation movement. One petition, probably Baptist in origin, "asserted that religion was not absolutely essential to good morals";[10] another maintained that "the exclusion of any religion from the assessment plan . . . made what should have been a state support of morality for the benefit of society a discriminating religious measure."[11] Such petitions helped mightily to bring legislative support back of Madison's fight.

A final factor which helped to bring Madison's plans to fruition was the multiplicity of sects. There were four major religious groups in Virginia—Episcopal, Methodist, Presbyterian, and Baptist. In their jealousies of each other lay an important insurance policy; as Madison pointed out, "security for civil rights must be the same as that for religious rights; it consists in the one case in a multiplicity of interests and in the other in a multiplicity of sects."[12]

2

It is probably true that Madison and Jefferson were not familiar with the writings of Roger Williams, yet it does not follow that they did not know his doctrines. They were exceedingly familiar with Baptist views on religious liberty which had been expressed in hundreds of petitions and memorials presented to the state legislature. It is perfectly possible that some of their ideas stemmed thus indirectly from Williams. They were also undoubtedly much influenced by Locke, Montesquieu, and other European writers. The view that the functions of church and state are essentially distinct is found in Locke, as it is in the following phrases of Madison: ". . . the bill implies either that the civil magistrate is a competent judge of religious truths, or that he may employ religion as an engine of civil policy. The first is an arrogant pretension . . .; the second, an unhallowed perversion of the means of salvation."[13] But Locke would never have maintained, as did Jefferson (and as had Williams), that "our civil rights have no dependence on our religious opinions."[14] Nor would Montesquieu have agreed that uniformity in religion is undesirable even if attainable.[15] It seems, therefore, that the ideas of religious liberty and separation espoused by Madison and Jefferson did not spring from any single source.

These ideas were an amalgam containing nothing particularly new, but they were stated forcefully and in terms calculated to appeal to the revolutionary American mind.

Fundamentally these ideas expressed a rationalistic view of human nature: morality derives from the nature of humanity, not from specific religious beliefs. Jefferson remarked:

Reading, reflection and time have convinced me that the interests of society require observation of those moral precepts only in which all religions agree. . . . The practice of morality being necessary for the well-being of society, he [the Creator] has taken care to impress its precepts so indelibly on our hearts that they shall not be effaced by the subtleties of our brain.[16]

From this it followed that the religious beliefs of any individual make no difference to social morality. Since no harm could accrue to society, the state could have no interest in the religious beliefs of its citizens, nor had it any power to meddle with them. They were personal affairs between God and man. If my neighbor's beliefs will take him to Hell, that makes no difference to me if he is otherwise a good neighbor. "It does me no injury for my neighbor to say there are twenty gods, or no god. It neither picks my pocket nor breaks my leg."[17] "The Religion . . . of every man must be left to the conviction and conscience of every man; and it is the right of every man to exercise it as these may dictate."[18]

Here emerges the idea of natural rights, which Jefferson possibly derived from his intensive study of pre-Norman English law. If it makes no difference to society what I believe, then I have a natural right to believe as I please and within certain limits to act on my beliefs. Coupled with the social compact theory prevalent in Virginia, this natural right becomes "unalienable."

Our rulers can have no authority over such natural rights. . . . The rights of conscience we never submitted, we could not submit.[19]
We are free to declare, and do declare, that the rights hereby asserted are of the natural rights of mankind, . . .[20]
If all men are by nature equally free and independent, all men are to be considered as entering society on equal conditions, as relinquishing no more, and therefore retaining no less, one than another of their natural rights; above all are they to be considered as

retaining an *equal* title to the free exercise of religion according to the dictates of conscience.[21]

This doctrine of natural rights was a natural prelude to a belief in the utter separation of the state from religion. Jefferson was particularly uncompromising on this point. He was explicit where even Williams had been implicit—that the public schools could not give religious education. As one of the board of visitors he therefore caused the elimination of religion instruction at William and Mary College while it was under state control in 1779.[22] The plan which he developed for the University of Virginia, often pointed to as evidence that he favored public support of religious education, was a concession to the necessity of gaining public support; and it really involved no sacrifice of principle, for the religious classes were not to be operated by the university nor was attendance to be required; the university actually was to contribute little but acquiescence.[23]

Further evidence of Jefferson's principles is the fact that he even went so far as to refuse, as President, to declare fast or thanksgiving days.[24] These were for their day extreme applications of separation, not agreeable to much of the populace. But there seems to have been great public support for the less radical applications of the theory, as is evidenced by the large number of petitions to the Virginia legislature favoring the Act for Religious Freedom.

Jefferson cited with approval Montesquieu's dictum that while civil law has the general welfare of society in view, religious law has only that of the individual, and therefore religious law is not always adaptable for use as civil law.[25] Neither Madison nor Jefferson accepted the view—popular among some religious groups today—that the state is a Christian institution or that Christianity is a part of the common law. Jefferson studied and wrote at length to disprove this.[26] To establish Christianity, whether or not it was the true religion, would be to offer carte blanche to any state to establish any religion, which principle Jefferson said "hath established and maintained false religions over the greatest part of the world, and through all time."[27] Madison agreed.[28]

The Act for Religious Freedom must be interpreted in the light of what its two greatest proponents believed and tried to accomplish through it. Madison wrote that the act "extinguished forever the ambitious hope of making laws for the human mind."[29] Jefferson was more explicit in discussing the act. He wrote:

Where the preamble declares, that coercion is a departure from the plan of the holy author of our religion, an amendment was proposed, by inserting the word "Jesus Christ," so that it should read, "a departure from the plan of Jesus Christ, the holy author of our religion"; the insertion was rejected by a great majority in proof that they meant to comprehend, within the mantle of its protection, the Jew and the Gentile, the Christian and the Mahometan, the Hindoo, and Infidel of every denomination.[30]

That this is the correct interpretation of the act is indicated by Nevins's comment that it was viewed by its opponents "as completely subversive of religious interests,"[31] and by the fact that as early as 1779 a bill which would have explicitly established Christianity as the state religion was defeated.[32]

3

The progress of other states toward religious liberty requires only brief notice, for nowhere except in the writings of Madison and Jefferson was the theory thoroughly explored. Most of the other states lagged somewhat behind Virginia because of several factors. In no other state, for instance, were the political leaders so insistent on religious liberty. In New England the established churches, not being organically connected with England, did not suffer as greatly during the Revolution as did the Anglican church; thus they retained more vitality with which to fight off the attacks of libertarians. In other states the fear of a moral decline or of an inflow of Catholics or non-Christians was influential. But everywhere the multiplicity of sects, the prevalence of religious indifference, and the spread of "natural religion" produced their effects. By 1800 only the Congregational establishments in New England, much weakened, still maintained themselves, and even these institutions were to be relatively shortlived. Their downfall was largely a matter of politics; it coincided with the death of the Federalist party and the triumph of Jeffersonianism. The end came in Vermont in 1807, Connecticut 1818, New Hampshire 1819, Maine 1820, and Massachusetts 1833.[33]

4

With the adoption of the federal Constitution it became necessary
to think about safeguarding the rights of citizens, not only as against
their state governments, but as against a national government as
well. Some individuals thought that such protection was contained
in the Constitution as it was originally adopted. This idea was based
on two factors: the prohibition of any religious test for federal
office in Article VI and the assumed lack of power of Congress
to act on any subject not expressly mentioned in the document.
James Madison, the chief architect of the Constitution, held this
view, as did Edmund Randolph. In the Virginia ratification convention
Randolph maintained that prohibition of a test "puts all sects on
the same footing. A man of abilities and character, of any sect whatever, may be admitted to any office."[34]

Many others, however, were reluctant to accept the Constitution
without a specific bill of rights including separation of church and
state. The battle on this point was particularly bitter in Virginia,
where Patrick Henry and George Mason were unalterably opposed
to any constitution not containing a bill of rights. Jefferson, from
Paris, eventually suggested that the Constitution, being on the whole
an acceptable document, be accepted with a pledge that a bill of
rights be secured after the formation of the new government.[35]

Madison, as has been suggested, put little trust in bills of rights,
relying primarily on the multiplicity of sects to maintain separation:

In Virginia I have seen the bill of rights violated in every instance
where it has been opposed to a popular current. . . . It is well
known that a religious establishment would have taken place in
that State, if the Legislative majority had found, as they expected,
a majority of the people in favor of the measure; and I am persuaded
that if a majority of the people were now of one sect, the measure
would still take place, and on narrower ground than was then
proposed.[36]

Madison also feared, and with reason, that any explicit amendment which could be obtained would be less liberal than he wished;
he preferred to rely on the broader grounds which he believed were
implicit in the Constitution already:

69

There is great reason to fear that a positive declaration of some of the most essential rights could not be obtained in the requisite latitude. I am sure that the rights of conscience, in particular, if submitted to public definition, would be narrowed much more than they are likely ever to be by an assumed power. One of the objections in New England was, that the Constitution, by prohibiting religious tests, opened a door for Jews, Turks, and infidels.[37]

Jefferson replied that "half a loaf is better than no bread. If we cannot secure all our rights, let us secure what we can," and added (strangely for one who did not ordinarily believe in judicial review) that a positive declaration of rights was important because of "the legal check which it puts into the hands of the judiciary" which, if independent, would not be affected by popular commotion.[38]

The necessity of getting the Constitution ratified indicated a concession by Madison; he took advantage of this fact to cut the ground out from under those who, like Henry, were using the absence of a bill of rights to cover for opposition to the Constitution itself. Madison therefore promised that he would press for a bill of rights as soon as the Constitution was adopted. At the first session of the new Congress he set out to redeem his pledge.[39]

At first he envisaged amendments which would not only have enacted substantially all of the Virginia Declaration of Rights and the Act for Religious Freedom, but would also have been a prohibition against *state* violations of religious rights—a point strangely neglected by later commentators.[40] As he had predicted, however, less liberal sentiment in Congress forced changes in his proposal. The restriction on the states was naturally opposed by states which still had religious establishments; eventually it was eliminated. The clause as regards the federal government was kept but was rendered innocuous and, worse, ambiguous in its final wording, which was apparently that proposed by the Massachusetts conservative Fisher Ames.[41]

The First Amendment as thus adopted contains the charter of religious liberty in the United States. Its exact meaning, then, is of utmost importance. It is incumbent upon us to try to understand what Congress actually meant to enact. Unfortunately the paucity of records makes this extremely difficult. No agreement has been reached by those who have studied the problem. It is obvious that the clause

"Congress shall make no law respecting an establishment of religion or prohibiting the free exercise thereof" is not as explicit as the Act for Religious Freedom written by Jefferson. Even so, a good case can be made for the belief that it was intended to secure the same object. It seems unlikely that Madison would have accepted the amendment with good grace had he not thought so. It is probable that he still relied heavily upon the prohibition of test oaths; and he may also have felt that the very ambiguity of the amendment would make liberal interpretation possible (apparently he felt that later generations would so interpret it).[42] His letter to Washington indicates inferentially that he shared the Baptist attitude on this point, and the Baptist attitude is of importance coming as it did from the most extreme religious advocates of liberty of conscience. "One of the principle leaders of the Baptists lately sent me word that the amendments had entirely satisfied the disaffected of his sect, and that it would appear in their subsequent conduct."[43]

The Baptist attitude on the amendment was further clarified by the statement of their Virginia leader John Leland, who said that it permitted "every man [to] speak freely without fear, maintaining the principles that he believes, [and to] worship according to his own faith either one god, three gods or no god or twenty gods, and let government protect him in doing so."[44]

Jefferson thought of the amendment in very uncompromising terms. He wrote that it built "a wall of separation between Church and State."[45] When he became President he refused to proclaim fast or thanksgiving days on grounds of unconstitutionality as well as of principle:

I consider the government of the United States as interdicted by the Constitution from intermeddling with religious institutions, their doctrines, discipline, or exercises. This results not only from the provision that no law shall be made respecting the establishment of free exercise of religion, but from that also which reserves to the States the powers not delegated to the United States. Certainly, no power to prescribe any religious exercise, or to assume authority in religious discipline, had been delegated to the General Government. . . . Fasting and prayer are religious exercises; the enjoining them an act of discipline . . . civil powers alone have been given to the President of the United States, and no authority to direct the religious exercises of his constituents.[46]

Further evidence of the meaning of the amendment may be gleaned from the prevailing spirit of the times which was distinctly secular as compared with the periods preceding and following them. The growth of deism and skepticism in late colonial and early national times has been many times remarked. Contacts with the British and French soldiery in the French-Indian and Revolutionary wars aided the spread of such doctrines. As early as 1759 Ezra Stiles had contended that "instead of the Controversies of Orthodoxy & Heresy, we shall soon be called to defence of the Gospel itself."[47]

It should be emphasized, perhaps, that at most not many Americans were deists. While such influential figures as Thomas Paine, Thomas Jefferson, George Mason, Ethan Allen, John Adams, and Benjamin Franklin have often been regarded as deists, there is no evidence that the masses of the population ever went to such an extreme. What is contended here is first that the influence of deism was great because it was concentrated in the groups which provided political leadership, and second that the populace as a whole was just not very much interested in religion, a fact which, if it did not favor the health of churches, nevertheless did indicate a spirit which could accept Jefferson's interpretation of the meaning of the First Amendment.

American deism was a rationalistic belief in a natural religion and a natural law. Extreme deists were likely to be "anti-clerical, anti-ecclesiastical, anti-scriptural, anti-authoritarian." With Paine they "found an adequate revelation of God in the constitution of nature." Such beliefs led to a tendency to divorce natural law from its medieval connection with divine law; it became instead a secularized belief in some sort of universal harmony, often with an admixture of relativism—a belief that instead of "a body of self-evident principles assumed to have a social end," reason could derive the principles *from* the end. "God retires into the background, where instead of creating human institutions, he lays down the guiding principles by which men create their own."

Such ideas of natural law and rights, whether held by deists or

72

Christians, provided a foundation for the Declaration of Independence, the attitude of which toward "religion in general might be described as that of friendly neutrality." There was a tendency to accept only the "reasonable" elements of Christianity such as "Christian" morality, and to leave to the churches the belief in revelation. Many deists, and many Christians too, would have agreed with Roger Williams that "there was absolutely no such thing under the gospel as a Christian state."[48]

The last half of the eighteenth century was the most skeptical era of American history, and while the intellectuals led the movement, they must have received some support from the common people. One estimate of church membership in 1775, for instance, is that nowhere in the colonies was membership in excess of 35 per cent of the population; another puts New England church membership at only one in five.[49] Deism and skepticism were rife in the colleges; Harvard, Yale, Dartmouth, New Jersey (Princeton), William and Mary—all were hotbeds of skepticism.

None of the first four presidents of the United States belonged to a church; two, Jefferson and Adams, were in some degree deists. Adams led the unsuccessful fight for separation in Massachusetts in 1820, even though he was eighty years old. The religious views of Washington are not known with any precision, although Jefferson quotes with some relish Benjamin Rush's belief based on information received from Gouverneur Morris that the first President was not a Christian. He astutely refrained from references to Christianity in his public pronouncements, beyond speaking of its "benign influence."[50]

Adams proposed in the Massachusetts Constitutional Convention of 1820 that the test oath be eliminated and equality extended in that state to "all men of all religions,"[51] and he also favored the end of blasphemy laws because, he said, "What free inquiry, when a writer must surely encounter a risk of fine or imprisonment for adducing any arguments for investigation into the divine authority of those books [of the Bible]? . . . Books that cannot bear examination, certainly ought not to be established as divine inspiration by penal laws."[52]

Madison's theories have already been examined. He was certainly anticlerical, but he probably was a Christian, although belonging to no church. The liberality of view in this period is pointed up by the fact that modern political scientists agree that today an avowed non-believer would have little chance of attaining the presidency, and active church attendance is considered a great political asset.

A final bit of evidence which may help to indicate that the Constitution did not intend the establishment of any religion, not even general Christianity, is the treaty with Tripoli negotiated in 1796 under the administration of the very men who had drafted the Constitution. This treaty states in Article XI that "The government of the United States of America is not in any sense founded on the Christian religion; . . . it has in itself no character of enmity against the laws, religion, or tranquillity of Musselmen."[53]

It seems, thus, that religious sentiment in the United States from 1775 to 1880 was liberal enough to lend credit to Jefferson's "wall of separation" dictum. The country was during those years less specifically "Christian" than at any time before or since.

It should also be emphasized that the diversity of religious groups in the United States, as Madison realized, was an important factor in the acceptance of separation; but such a factor would not operate against the establishment of general Christianity, since all these groups were Christian.

In spite of all the evidence adduced above, the ambiguity of phrasing of the First Amendment has given rise to another view of its meaning. This view can, according to its proponents, be supported by arguments at least as strong as the ones already used herein. In brief it holds that the United States is and always was a Christian nation and that therefore it is impossible to suppose that the Constitution should not take that fact into consideration by at least favoring religion in general or at most supporting Protestant Christian religion. It flows from this theory that Christianity (or alternatively religion in general or Protestantism in general) is regarded as the established religion of the nation and that the only thing the First Amendment does is to forbid the establishment of any particular sect and to prohibit governmental interference with the rights of conscience. My position, as stressed above, is that this argument is historically false because it assumes a specifically Christian character which may not have existed at the time the Constitution was written.

74

Its proponents have taken a social situation which admittedly existed in the United States from 1800 or so and have projected it back to the Revolutionary period when it did *not* exist, or at least did not exist so strongly.[54]

The argument may be false even if one grants its historical premise that the nation was prevailingly Christian in 1790. For there is no reason why good, even fanatic, Christians might not as part of their faith renounce any support from the state, as Roger Williams, Isaac Backus, James Iredell, and the Baptists and Quakers generally urged. In their view the state is non-Christian and nonreligious; if the people are Christian it is because they have freely chosen to be so, not because any law or Constitution has so enacted. As Williams so forcefully put it:

There goes many a ship to sea, with many hundred souls in one ship, whose weal and woe is common, and is a true picture of a commonwealth, or a human combination or society. It hath fallen out sometimes, that both papists and protestants, Jews and Turks, may be embarked in one ship; upon which supposal I affirm, that all the liberty of conscience, that ever I pleaded for, turns upon these two hinges—that none of the papists, protestants, Jews, or Turks, be forced to come to the ship's prayers or worship, nor compelled from their own particular prayers or worship, if they practice any. I further add, that I never denied, that notwithstanding this liberty, the commander of this ship ought to command the ship's course, yea, and also command that justice, peace and sobriety, be kept and practiced, both among the seamen and all the passengers. If any of the seamen refuse to perform their services, or passengers to pay their freight; if any refuse to help, in person or purse, towards the common charges or defence; if any refuse to obey the common laws and orders of the ship, concerning their common peace or preservation; if any shall mutiny and rise up against their commanders or officers, because all are equal in Christ, therefore no masters nor officers, no laws nor orders, nor corrections nor punishments;—I say, I never denied, but in such cases, whatever is pretended, the commander or commanders may judge, resist, compel and punish such transgressors, according to their deserts and merits.[55]

While in some of its aspects Williams's doctrine may be extreme, his idea that the "ship of state" cannot be Christian, but only the people aboard the ship, and that the governance of the ship will be legitimate whether or not it is framed in Christian terms, can be echoed by many a devout Christian. In substance such an argument says: The United States was not a Christian nation in 1790 because neither it nor any other nation has *ever* been a Christian nation.

Thus did the state and national constitutions erect barriers against the encroachment of the state upon the province of the church and the individual conscience and that of the church upon the political authority. How frail and yet how durable these barriers have proved will be the subject of the next chapter.

4

Testing the Constitutional Principle
1800-1958

T HE NINETEENTH CENTURY witnessed a religious revival in America. A country which had seen in the late eighteenth century an astonishing spread of skepticism and indifference became once more a stronghold of religion. This revival meant that the new principles of religious liberty written into the American constitution were to be subjected to severe strain.

1

It is not true, although it has often been so assumed, that the writing of the constitutional provisions meant the end of mankind's long struggle against bigotry and intolerance. In truth, the battle was merely shifted to a different level. Where the seventeenth and eighteenth centuries had seen a Christian sect on the defensive against other Christian groups, the nineteenth and twentieth centuries have seen largely a defense of Christianity itself against the granting of equality to non-Christians.

Christians tended increasingly to assume that this was a Christian nation and that therefore the state had the right and duty to promote

Christianity and to refuse, at the least, to promote anything else. In the same way two centuries earlier England was considered an Anglican nation, France a Catholic nation, Massachusetts a Puritan domain. The difference was that the religious-liberty clauses in American fundamental law made such an assumption difficult in most cases and practically impossible in some. Nevertheless, Christian sentiment in general always interpreted any constitutional provision referring to "religion" or "sect" as if it had the word "Christian" prefixed. Needless to say, if a constitution enjoined a state from refusing the franchise to any "sect," such an interpretation could be used to destroy the political rights of the Jews or of the religiously indifferent.

Such are the ways of conservatism. Forced to withdraw from one battlement, it does not surrender but lives to fight again from another. Its greatest weakness is that it never learns from previous defeats; it always uses the same arguments and the same weapons. In England, as we have seen, first the Baptist, then the Quaker, then the Unitarian was opposed, each on the grounds that anyone with such beliefs could not be a good member of society and that the toleration of such beliefs would destroy the social fabric. Thus political rights could not be granted to such as believed in these doctrines. Religion was always equated with civic morality and citizenship. When this position became too absurd to defend any longer, the Baptist, the Quaker, the Unitarian were in turn accepted, as eventually all Christian sects have been accepted, with no apparent loss to public morality. Religious conservatism then fell back; but the same argument was and is used to defend its new positions. It is now said that the non-Christian, the infidel, the deist, and the atheist cannot be good citizens.[1]*

This in brief is the story of the struggle for religious liberty since 1800. Constitutional provisions have prevented the outright prohibition of, or flagrant discrimination against, the unwanted beliefs—at least in most cases. But the religious conservative, despite such legal handicaps, remains at the old stand peddling the same old wares, now slightly shopworn but still, apparently, salable to the gullible.

* Notes to this chapter begin on page 164.

2

The interest of the democratic state in the education of its future citizens has never been contested. Democracy perhaps more than any other form of political organization demands a high level of knowledge of public affairs on the part of the populace. The rise of democratic government, therefore, has been accompanied by the development of the state educational system. If it is legitimate or even necessary for the state to interest itself in the education of its citizens, it seems legitimate and necessary for it to provide the required facilities and to ascertain that the job is well done. The aim of public education, then, is to produce citizens who can function successfully in the democratic system and who have the skills to earn their living in ways which will contribute to the democratic society.

At the same time the introduction of "public" education inevitably raised problems of church and state which had not existed previously. For if the public schools conduct programs of religious indoctrination, the force of the state is being put behind religion in a way which many think is contrary to our constitutional and philosophical belief in separation. Yet in modern times it has become difficult for the churches to reach their children without the aid of the coercive arm of the state; consequently there has been much pressure for just this type of state aid through the school system.

Massachusetts Bay Colony was not exactly a democracy. But its government early took the lead in providing for the education of its children. It is significant that it was the state which took this step, not the church, for it marked a first step away from exclusively church-sponsored education. It is true that in a church-state, such as Massachusetts was, education for citizenship would inevitably include religious education, and in a predominant role, for as we have seen, citizenship was conceived in religious terms. This was recognized in the 1654 law on education: "It greatly concerns the welfare of this country that the youth thereof be educated, not only in good literature, but sound doctrine."[2] In Massachusetts the "sound doctrine" was so important that the "good literature" meant mostly the Bible and commentaries thereon. In most towns the local preacher taught the school, and always the clergy exercised "supervisory power" over education.[3] As Smith comments, it was not the three R's which were taught, but the four: "Reading, 'Riting, 'Rithmetic, and Religion."[4] In fact, religion was considered to be of such pre-eminent importance that education was largely thought to have for its object the inculcation of the religious knowledge necessary for good Puritan citizenship. Not only good ministers, but good public officials, must be "learned and godly men."[5] The result was that Harvard College, a state-controlled institution, assumed the character of a theological seminary.

But the really important aspect of the Massachusetts schools is that they were state controlled, not that they were religiously oriented. For state control meant that a religious orientation would last only so long as the state itself was so oriented. Religious education was at the mercy of the state. Thus as time went on and the "standing order" weakened and died, the schools lost more and more of their religious tone. The secularized state begot a secularized school; and the sects, if they wished to educate youth in their sectarian beliefs, must perforce do it themselves. By 1800 it was generally true that public education in Massachusetts had lost its sectarian tone.

The legal separation of church and state, as Jefferson saw, logically required also a separation of the church from public education. But the resurgent forces of religion in the nineteenth century took the view that (again, since this was a Christian nation) separation did not bar Christian religious instruction in the schools, but only *sectarian* religious teaching. Thus they held that the precepts and beliefs common to all Christians might properly be subjects of public education. The histories of education and religion in Massachusetts, Virginia, and North Carolina, which bring out the struggle between Jeffersonian principles of separation and the "established Christianity" viewpoint, establish facts which were generally true throughout all the states. The forces of religion pressed, often successfully, for religion classes, Bible reading, the Lord's Prayer, and other religious exercises in the public schools. Their success was not limited to the slow-moving former Puritan colonies; it was notable even in Virginia, the home of the Act for Religious Freedom, and was accomplished there even though that statute was and is still on the books. In fact, the nineteenth century saw the South in general accept the conservative view, while Massachusetts was to take her place among the more progressive states. This remarkable reversal was largely due to the rapid immigration of Irish Catholics into the United States. This immigration was directed mostly to the northern cities.

The tenet that general Christianity was to be taught in the schools was all very well as long as most people were Protestants, for Protestants could, with some difficulty, agree on the principles to be taught. But in a district where there were many Catholics, one of two things would happen: either no agreement could be reached as to what principles should be taught, or (if the Catholics were strong enough) general Christianity became Catholic rather than Protestant. To avoid such a calamity the Protestants gave up formalized religious education in the schools and developed instead the Sunday School run under their own church auspices. In the South, on the other hand, few Catholics were found except in scattered places; Protestantism did not, therefore, find such renunciation necessary.

3

The fact that the First Amendment to the United States Constitution was an injunction against only the federal government prevented the national courts and government from being involved in the struggle over separation before the Civil War. The adoption of the Fourteenth Amendment did not immediately change the situation, due to the emasculation of the amendment's privileges and immunities clause by the Supreme Court in the Slaughterhouse and succeeding cases.[6] Nevertheless, the federal courts were occasionally called upon to rule on the meaning of the religious clauses in the First Amendment. The most important instance was the question of Mormon polygamy. Since most Mormons lived in Utah which was then a federal territory, any action against polygamy had to be taken by the national government. Congress precipitated the controversy by passing an act making plural marriage a criminal offense. When Reynolds, a Mormon, was convicted under this act, the Supreme Court was forced to rule on its validity under the First Amendment. As far as we are concerned the major questions involved were two: was Christianity the law of the land and did polygamy therefore violate it? and did the First Amendment prohibit the government from regulating such acts as plural marriage when they were performed as a part of a religious belief?

The first question was sidestepped in Chief Justice Waite's opinion for rather obvious reasons. In the first place, the court might have had a hard time upholding the act on the basis that Christianity was the law of the land, since (as we have seen) the evidence on the point is conflicting. In the second place, a declaration that polygamy was a violation of Christian principles would be open to grave attack, since the Mormons are Christians and as such have as much right to define Christian morality as any other sect. How could a court pick and choose between the doctrines of varying Christian sects as to which was the law of the land?

Consequently the Court was forced to rule directly upon the constitutionality of the statute. Was the prohibition of polygamy a violation of the religious liberty guaranteed by the First Amendment? In the nineteenth century, or even today, a court could conveniently come to only one conclusion. The Chief Justice quoted Jefferson to the effect that the civil officers may interfere with religious practices when they "break out into overt acts against peace and good order." He went on to indicate that polygamy had always been considered "odious" in the Western World and was punishable at common law and that it had always been an offense against society in this country. Furthermore, he concluded, marriage is a civil contract and as such may be regulated by the state. On these grounds the antipolygamy statute and the good order and peace of society were maintained.[7]

This case brings out clearly the problem with which John Locke and his predecessors failed to deal: who is to decide the issue when the civil and religious spheres come into conflict? Locke, we have seen, dismissed the issue by saying that it would seldom if ever arise, but the Supreme Court could not get around it so easily. The answer of the Court is implicit but obvious: when the interests of the state and those of religion conflict, the state must decide whether the question involves political stability to a great enough degree to prohibit the religious practice in controversy. Obviously the extent of governmental interference under such a condition depends not so much on any constitutional restriction as it does on the sense of restraint and devotion to liberty of the political authorities who make the decision. The value of the separation principle, however, is that it reduces the area of conflict between the political and the religious, and thus reduces also the number of conflicts. It cannot eliminate conflict, but it can minimize it. From the political viewpoint such conflicts *should* be minimized, because they may arouse passions which will threaten political stability. There can be no doubt that in the Reynolds case, regardless of the correctness of the Court's views as to the immorality of polygamy or the constitutionality of the law, the decision reached was the only one politically possible in view of the prevailing American hostility to plural marriage. The threat to peace and good order, in other words, came not from the practice itself, but from the passions of opposition it aroused.[8]

In 1891 the Supreme Court stuck the judicial neck out somewhat further when, in ruling that a church had the right to import the minister of its choice from abroad despite immigration regulations, the Court speaking through Justice Brewer averred not only that "this is a religious nation" but that "this is a Christian nation." He based this conclusion on an analysis of the wording of several of our most conservative state constitutions which, he said, "speak the voice of the entire people."[9] This seeming victory for the forces of Christianity—for such a declaration could be used to sanction many breaches of the separation rule—was, however, largely vitiated by two aspects of Brewer's opinion. First, the declaration was an obiter dictum, a judicial aside. The statement that this is either a religious or a Christian nation was not essential to the decision reached; it was surplus verbiage. Second, the Court's opinion indicated that Jewish ministers as well as Christian could be freely imported, thus leaving it in doubt whether Brewer meant that this is a Christian nation or merely a religious one. In any case the dictum has not been picked up by succeeding courts, although it is often cited by wishful thinkers.

While the Supreme Court was thus kept out of the religious field except where federal statutes were concerned, the state courts had to bear the burden of deciding whether religious instruction in the public schools was a violation of state constitutional provisions, whether the state constitution or common law made the state a Christian nation, and so on. The decisions reached are so widely conflicting that no clear pattern can be derived from their study. But some of them were important because they contained opinions about the separation theory which went far beyond the language of pure law and entered into the different realm of political theory.

In a bit of strange confusion the Supreme Judicial Court of Maine in 1854 declared that the state "knows no religion," and continued, "It regards the Pagan and the Mormon, the Brahmin and the Jew, the Swedenborgian and the Buddhist, the Catholic and the Quaker, as all possessing equal rights."[10] After such a ringing pronouncement of the separation doctrine, the court's decision is a study in contrast, for it upheld the reading of the King James Version of the Bible in the public schools against a Catholic protest! The grounds were that the Bible was used merely for reading instruction, just as a book on Greek mythology might be used. The fact that the reading of this particular Bible, a sacred book to all Protestants, was also a religious act was overlooked by the court. It ended by practically nullifying its own previous statement and the state constitutional provision as well, when it concluded, "[The] State is governed by its own views of duty. The right or wrong of the State, is the right or wrong as declared by legislative acts constitutionally passed . . . [therefore no citizen] is to be legally absolved from obedience because they [the laws] may conflict with his conscientious views of religious duty and right."[11]

The Nebraska Supreme Court also took the view that reading the Bible need not be an act of worship. "Certainly the Iliad may be read in the schools without inculcating a belief in the Olympic divinities, and the Koran may be read without preaching the Moslem faith. Why may not the Bible also be read without indoctrinating children . . . ?"[12] The court believed that the Bible could be used without indoctrination; but the sentiment of Nebraskans would probably not tolerate the reading of many other books even as literature—let us say, the books of Mary Baker Eddy or the *Book of Mormon!* Some educational authorities believe that nothing can be taught without indoctrination either for or against; and most congressmen, at least, would seriously question the reading, as literature, of Marx or Lenin. Catholics who protest the reading of the Protestant Bible are not so naive on this point as the Protestants whose Bible is being read. And the Nebraska court like that of Maine had preceded its bit of legal wisdom with a statement of exceedingly liberal sentiment. "The suggestion that it is the duty of government to teach religion has no basis whatever in the constitution or laws of this state, nor in the history of our people."[13]

Such cases could be multiplied almost indefinitely without any particular gain. If this were a treatise on constitutional law it might be necessary to do so, but since our interest is not in legal application but in political wisdom, it does not seem desirable.[14]

Other courts have been somewhat more consistent in their application of the theory of separation. In an Ohio case upholding Sunday closing laws (but on the basis of the state's police power rather than on religious grounds[15]), the court stood squarely for complete separation:

Neither Christianity, nor any other system of religion is a part of the law of this state. We sometimes hear it said that all religions are tolerated in Ohio; but the expression is not strictly accurate— much less accurate is it to say, that one religion is a part of our law, and all others only tolerated. It is not by mere toleration that every individual here is protected in his belief or disbelief. He rests not upon the leniency of government, or the liberality of any class or sect of men, but upon his natural and indefeasible rights of conscience, which, in the language of the constitution, are beyond the control or interference of any human authority.[16]

The Ohio courts followed up this decision with another preventing school authorities from requiring religious instruction in the state's public schools. The court, in a long obiter dictum, argued cogently against such instruction:

The real claim here is, that by "religion," in this clause of the constitution, is meant "Christian religion." . . .

.   .   .   .

If by this generic word "religion" was really meant "the Christian religion," why was it not plainly so written? . . . When they speak of "religion" they must mean the religion of man, and not the religion of any *class* of men. When they speak of "all men" having certain rights, they cannot mean merely "all Christian men." . . .

The only foundation—rather, the only excuse—for the proposition, that Christianity is part of the law of this country, is the fact that it is a Christian country, and that its constitutions and laws were made by a Christian people. . . . [But] a form of religion that cannot live under equal and impartial laws ought to die, and sooner or later must die.

.   .   .   .

The state can have no religious opinions. . . .

[This] means masterly inactivity on the part of the state, except for the purpose of keeping the conflict free, and preventing the violation of private rights or of the public peace.[17]

Other state courts have taken much the same attitude. The Wisconsin court condemned religious instruction in state institutions even when those objecting could be excused from class. This results, said the court, in a loss of caste and a subjection to "reproach and insult." "The practice in question tends to destroy the equality of the pupils which the constitution seeks to establish and protect."[18] A concurring opinion stressed the completeness of the separation which the state constitution enjoins. The schools, said Justice Orton, are Godless "in the same sense that the executive, legislative, and administrative departments are Godless."[19]

The Louisiana court agreed that even when a pupil may be excused from a Bible-reading class, discrimination exists. The Bible is a religious book, and "it is not adapted for use as a textbook . . . without regard to its religious character."[20]

These cases could also be multiplied greatly, but again such a course is needless.[21] Enough has been said to indicate that the struggle between the church and the state is not over. The cases, taken as a body, represent a reaffirmation of the doctrines of Roger Williams and of Thomas Jefferson. More important, they illustrate the adaptation of theory to specific questions of law. A theory which cannot stand the test of application is foredoomed. Thus it may be said that the judicial decisions which apply rigorously, rather than those which attempt to limit, the theory of separation constitute not only an application of, but a positive contribution to, the theory

86

itself. Throughout the nineteenth century, then, it was the state judiciaries which made the main additions to the separation theory—additions which, because they were legally enforced, buttressed the theory.

4

In the twentieth century the pendulum of constitutional interpretation has swung to the federal courts on the vital questions of religious liberty. The Supreme Court of the United States opened the way for this development when it evaded the Slaughterhouse case holding on the privileges and immunities clause of the Fourteenth Amendment. This development was foreshadowed by two decisions in 1923 which, without referring to the First Amendment, held that the "liberty" spoken of in the due-process clause of the Fourteenth includes religious liberty.[22] It was not until the so-called "Roosevelt Court" in the 1940's that the religious clauses of the First Amendment were specifically applied against the states under the wording of the Fourteenth.[23] From then on, however, it was assured that the important religious cases would be appealed to the federal Supreme Court. And they came in a flood.

In a case involving religious rights there are many lines of thought which a court can pursue in reaching its decision. None is either easy to apply or precise in its application. Judicial determination in this field is "case by case"; precedents do not often clearly apply. Which methods of reaching a conclusion are taken in any particular case is largely a result of the philosophy of the Court; and the philosophy of the Court (even in these days of disagreeing majorities) is an amalgam of the individual philosophies of the justices. Since 1940 the Court has almost unanimously adopted Madison's and Jefferson's theory of separation. There have been wide differences of opinion in each case, however, as to just what Jefferson's theory means and how it can be applied to present-day problems. The following is a survey of some of the methods available which have been used in the religious cases to help in the process of decision making.

1. *Historical.* In several cases the Court has made a determined

effort to base its decision on what the framers of the First Amendment meant to do. There is, as we have seen, much difference of opinion on this point. But the Court has, in general, adopted Thomas Jefferson's "wall of separation" theory, including (or .adding, as some critics claim) the idea that the state is barred from aiding one religion or all religions and from giving any preference to one over another, as Justice Black put it in his famous Everson case opinion.[24] In this case and the later McCollum case the Court has gone extensively into the business of making (or as Corwin puts it, remaking) history.[25] It has thoroughly examined the background of the First Amendment and has decided that Jefferson's theory was embodied in it. Although I believe this interpretation to be the correct one, it is unprovable and controversial and on the whole a poor basis for decision if used exclusively. There are several reasons for this.

First, the brevity of Congressional debate and the lack of writings on the question by the framers make any historical argument inconclusive and open to serious question. Second, the amendment was designed to outlaw practices which had existed before its writing, but there is no authoritative declaration of the specific practices at which it was aimed. And third, most of the modern religious-freedom cases turn on issues which were at most academic in 1789 and perhaps did not exist at all. Public education was almost nonexistent in 1789, and the question of religious education in public schools may not have been foreseen. And the use of loud-speakers in public parks was certainly not in the minds of the framers.[26]

For such reasons the historical argument can apply to most recent decisions only by implication. The justices, in short, must apply their own opinions of what Madison or Jefferson would think of the present-day problem if he were now alive—a process which is fraught with the possibility of error and which actually leaves the Court free to decide, as Justice Jackson once remarked, under "no law but our own prepossessions."[27]

Another objection which liberals may have to the use of the historical method is that in the hands of an illiberal court it may be actually dangerous to religious freedom. It can as well be used, even if one accepts Jefferson's theory of it, to limit freedom as to protect or enlarge it. As one writer trenchantly remarks,

The Founding Fathers were novices in the field of religious freedom, for they had come from a background of bigotry and lived in an era of intolerance. . . . It would be a strange commentary on the flexibility of our democratic government, if after 150 years of growth our concepts of freedom were limited to the narrow horizons of our forefathers. The First Amendment, if it is to keep step with the times, must give much wider protection than it did in 1789.[28]

Properly used, then, the historical method can provide no more explicit guide to decision than a set of broad outer limits within which the play of "our own prepossessions" or of public opinion may have a decisive influence.

2. *Political process.* In at least one case the Court has taken the view that it will not strike down state legislation except in flagrant cases so long as the remedial processes of government leave open the possibility of agitation for repeal. Justice Frankfurter strongly urged this view in his opinion in the first flag-salute cases in which he said:

Except where the transgression of constitutional liberty is too plain for argument, personal freedom is best maintained—so long as the remedial channels of the democratic process remain open and unobstructed—when it is ingrained in a people's habits and not enforced against popular policy by the coercion of adjudicated law.[29]

Frankfurter reiterated this view in his dissent in the second flag-salute case, in which the Court reversed itself and overruled the Gobitis decision.[30]

As to the merits of the argument, there is a good deal of truth and wisdom in Frankfurter's approval of the Holmesian dictum that experimentation should be permitted in the "insulated compartments" of the states. But Holmes was referring to economic experiment, not to civil liberties. In any case, the constitutional principle in civil-liberty questions is quite clear: the state is barred from "experimenting" with the liberties which the Constitution guarantees. In addition, while Frankfurter's faith in the democratic process is sincere and deeply felt, one may question its realism; his theory is very close to one of pure majority rule. In this connection he cited Madison and Jefferson as knowing "that minorities may disrupt society";[31] yet both these patriots also realized that *majorities* can disrupt society, too, by trampling on minority rights and privileges. This was the main, and in fact the only, reason for the inclusion of the Bill of Rights in the Constitution—an inclusion, as we have seen, which was pushed hardest by the most extreme democrats, men like Patrick Henry. The Bill of Rights can be meaningful as a constitutional protection only against the tyranny of a majority which might forget that inalienable rights belong to minorities as well as to majorities. To apply Frankfurter's theory might well be to make the Bill of Rights a complete nullity—an eventuality which Frankfurter would dislike as deeply as anyone on the Court.

3. *Minority protection.* It was his recognition of such a danger that led Justice Stone to make his lonely dissent to the Gobitis decision, a dissent which was to capture the majority in the Barnette case. Stone's thesis was that there are certain fundamental rights which are constitutionally protected from state violation and that the Court is duty bound to enforce these rights even if it means a limitation on governmental action. He objected to Frankfurter's idea because, he said, it meant "the surrender of the constitutional protection of the liberty of small minorities to the popular will," and he advanced a contrary theory that the constitutional provisions do, and were meant to, limit governmental action.[32]

The very fact that we have constitutional guaranties of civil liberties. and the specificity of their command where freedom of speech and of religion are concerned require some accommodation of the powers which government normally exercises. when no question of civil liberty is involved, to the constitutional demand that those liberties be protected against the action of government itself.[33]

His view was, in short, that national unity is a legitimate object of governmental action, but that such action cannot abrogate constitutional limitations.

Stone's argument seems philosophically more tenable than Frankfurter's, but it does not really solve the question in any particular case, since it gives no clue as to where civil liberty ends and legitimate governmental action begins. There is no doubt, for instance, that in the Mormon polygamy case religious liberty was denied and legislation approved; yet even Stone would not doubt the correctness of the decision. Stone's theory provides no touchstone. In each case the Court must still decide which interest under the situation of that particular case is paramount, that of political and social aims or that of civil liberty. It is this enduring necessity which makes liberty perpetually a thing which must be fought for, a thing which must be continually reasserted as one of the predominant values in the competition for supremacy. Liberty must compete with other values; and as far as the courts are concerned, the outcome of the competition depends not so much on a constitutional principle as on the philosophical theories of the judges.

4. *Preferred rights.* Another rule which has been enunciated by the Court, and which is also opposed to the Frankfurter theory, is that which holds that some rights have a preferred status and should invariably be protected by the courts. Frankfurter had maintained that legislation should be upheld if it could be considered reasonable, placing apparently the burden of proof on the aggrieved party. But Justice Murphy took up the cudgels against this doctrine. Religious liberty, he thought, was so sacred a privilege that the shoe should be put on the other foot. That is, in a case involving religious rights the state should be required to prove that its action, as regards the restriction of liberty, is reasonable. It will not do to prove its reasonableness as general legislation; it must be reasonable in its application to religious liberty. The presumption of the Court, said Murphy, should be that any violation of the rights guaranteed in the First Amendment is "prima facie invalid. Religious freedom is too sacred a right to be restricted or prohibited in any degree without convincing proof that a legitimate interest of the state is in grave danger."[34] This preferential treatment of the freedoms specified in the First Amendment is common, if largely implicit, with the Court in religious cases.[35]

Justice Murphy's doctrine seems to follow clearly from the idea of a bill of rights, for if such rights as are there enunciated were not considered more basic than others, why were they put there to begin with? Professor Meiklejohn has argued persuasively that the First Amendment is couched in absolute terms.[36] It seems apparent at the least that the very specification of rights contained in the

First Amendment implies their preference over the general activities of government; they were put there consciously in order to restrict governmental action, whether "reasonable" or not, which impinged upon the liberties of citizens. In matters where there is no specific constitutional prohibition, the usual court rule—often ignored by courts—is that there is a presumption of constitutionality and that if the law is considered by the Court to be a reasonable exercise of some legitimate governmental power, such as the police power, the law should be sustained. There is grave doubt, however, that such should be the case where there is a clause in the Constitution which *prohibits* governmental action, especially when the prohibition is couched in such absolute terms as those of the First Amendment. There is thus some value in Justice Murphy's contention that when such prohibitions are involved, a law should be considered invalid unless "convincing proof" of its necessity be offered. Some, like Frankfurter, would fear that legitimate state action would be made impossible by such an interpretation; this need not be the case, however. Even with a presumption of unconstitutionality it is still necessary for the Court to decide whether or not convincing proof has been offered. It is, in other words, the Court which must be convinced. A court made up of Frankfurters would doubtless be easier to convince than one made up of Murphys. The shift in emphasis would not be as important as the make-up of the Court. Again it is the judges rather than the rule of interpretation which are of fundamental importance.

Obviously, too, Justice Murphy's guide is not self-applicatory, for there may be wide variance, and usually there is, among opinions as to what may constitute a "legitimate interest of the state." Also, it might be added, differences could arise as to the meaning of "grave danger." Is the prevention of child labor a "legitimate interest of the state"? Undoubtedly it is. But does the use of children to pass out *Watchtower* pamphlets expose the state's interest to "grave danger"? The answer depends, once more, on the prepossessions of the judges. Is the regulation of street parades a legitimate interest? Or the prevention of doorbell ringing by ardent religionists?

Finally, one might ask, does Murphy really mean to say that *any* legitimate interest of the state if gravely endangered must be upheld

by the courts, even though it means an infringement of liberty? One
may seriously question the assumption that "order in public"—certainly a legitimate interest—should be allowed to override the right
of groups to meet in public parks, for instance. We are forced, as
in the previous points, to the conclusion that "rules" in the field
of religious rights are no rules at all and are as likely to prove
confusing as helpful.

5. *General applicability.* The Court has sometimes held that a
law of general applicability is valid, even though it interferes incidentally with religious liberties. This view is diametrically opposed
to that of Murphy discussed above, and the Court in each case must
decide which of the two it prefers. The result generally depends on
the Court's view of the importance of the legislation and the degree
to which it impinges upon liberty.

The rule of general applicability was stated forcefully by Justice
Frankfurter in the Gobitis case.

The religious liberty which the Constitution protects does not exclude
legislation of general scope not directed against doctrinal loyalties
of particular sects. . . . The mere possession of religious convictions
which contradict the relevant concerns of a political society does not
relieve the citizen from the discharge of political responsibilities.[37]

It is doubtful if most judges would follow Frankfurter as far
as these remarks seem to go. The validity of the argument, provided
it is properly qualified, is undeniable. Its application in a compulsory
vaccination case was undoubtedly wise.[38] But as applied in a flag-
salute or a streetlittering-ordinance case, it is of doubtful wisdom.[39]

The fact that Frankfurter gives no weight to the *importance,* as
distinct from the relevance, of the "concerns of a political society"
is cause for comment. It is probable that he does not actually mean
that *any* relevant concern expressed in a general law would be
sufficient to uphold the law regardless of how minor the subject
matter of the law may be. There is a vast difference between the
importance of laws regulating the holding of public meetings in
parks and of laws prohibiting plural marriages. Frankfurter's doctrine
gives no weight to such differences, however; it is enough that both
types of law are of "relevant concern" to society.

93

As stated earlier, it is also true that even an important *and* relevant concern may still not be enough to justify upholding a law, for the liberty involved may well be more important than the interest of the political society. The maintenance of patriotism through the use of a flag salute is no doubt important. But is it more important than the maintenance of religious freedom? No one, not even a Supreme Court justice, can answer such a question definitively. The law is not well adapted to weighing questions of values, and such a question is, par excellence, one calling for a discriminating value judgment.

That Frankfurter himself does not completely agree with his doctrine seems to be indicated by his Everson case dissent. No one would deny that safe transportation of pupils to school is a relevant concern of society; yet Justice Frankfurter agreed with his dissenting colleagues that such transportation could not be constitutionally provided to parochial school students.[40] Obviously more than mere "relevance" must be considered. All things that are of relevant concern are not thereby constitutional; if they were, our Bill of Rights would be deprived of much of its utility in protecting us from governmental interferences with our liberties.

Neither is the general scope of legislation a complete criterion of its constitutionality in religious cases. It is obvious that laws of general scope on their face may be used to discriminate against particular groups. Southern evasions of the Constitution's suffrage requirements are a case in point, and the courts have latterly been very cautious in approving such evasions. The application of the law, and not merely its scope, is of concern; and if a law of general scope *does in practice* work against "the doctrinal loyalties of particular sects," that is one factor which should be taken into consideration by the courts. Scope, relevance, and *importance and effect* are all part of the complex picture which the courts should consider before making decisions.

6. *Interference with liberty of others.* A sixth test that has been proposed is the degree to which an action impelled by religious conviction impinges upon the freedom of others. This test involves a balancing of freedoms. Justice Jackson proposed its use in his dissent in the Prince case; he suggested that limitations on religious

94

liberty should begin only when the actions affect those outside the religious group which condones or sanctions them.[41] This argument has gained some prominence because of the Supreme Court's refusal to use it in the released-time case. It requires an analysis of both freedom *from* and freedom *for*, as is well brought out in the controversy over that case.

The Court apparently felt that the freedom *from* any element of state coercion in religious matters is the most important factor. But others believe that their freedom *for* religious instruction is more important than the freedom from it of a few "atheists." This opinion has been advanced by one of America's leading constitutional authorities in the following words:

Have the parents of children who must for financial or other reasons attend the public schools no right to guide the education of their children, and hence no right to demand that the education available through the public schools shall not be purely secular? It would seem that the decision in the McCollum case amounts to a law prohibiting the "free exercise" of religion—a type of law which is in definite words banned by Amendment I![42]

And another prominent Catholic writer seconds it:

This case was different. It was a matter of one child and its parents against all the other children in the community. It was decided in favor of the one child, but in this kind of case, what, it can be asked, becomes of the freedom of religion of all the others? Before, it was always the power of the state that was restricted. Here, it is the freedom of other individual citizens that is denied.[43]

The last two sentences are certainly not true. The defeat of the assessment proposal in Virginia (reviewed in the previous chapter) had exactly the same effect as the defeat of the released-time religious-instruction program of Champaign, Illinois: certain religious groups lost the freedom to use the state as a prop for their beliefs. This seems to indicate that the posing of the issue as "freedom from versus freedom for" is not very meaningful, unless one asks, freedom from what? and freedom for what? Besides, no group of citizens, however large, can ask the state to do what the Constitution forbids it to do—unless the citizens first pass an amendment.

Again, laying aside the question of whether or not coercion did exist in the Champaign setup, it appears that the major question was whether the freedom of the McCollum boy (and of all others who may have been in like position) not to attend religious classes in public school on school time, or the freedom of other children so to attend religious classes, is the most valuable. Since, given the will on the part of the parents, children, and church, religious education can be secured outside the public schools, it would seem— once more assuming that coercion existed—that the first freedom was actually the one which most needed protection. At least the Supreme Court thought so by an (in those days unusual) over-whelming majority.[44]

Whatever the decision in a particular case may be, it is, I believe, obvious that the balancing of freedoms is a tricky thing and a job which courts of law are not well qualified to handle. Yet under the American constitutional system such questions inevitably present themselves to the courts. It is the judges' own value hierarchies which determine their answer, not a legal or constitutional principle.

7. *Clear and present danger.* The Supreme Court has at times attempted to apply the Holmes-Brandeis "clear and present danger" rule to religious-liberty cases. Since such cases in this country— thanks to separation of church and state—seldom if ever pose an actual threat to any government, the question resolves itself, not into a question of clear and present danger to the state, but into one of danger to some paramount interest the state feels bound to protect. Obviously this again means the weighing of values, not the application of principles of law. Justice Murphy used this concept, as well as that of preferred rights, in his Prince case dissent. The state, he said, had completely failed to prove the "existence of any grave or immediate danger to any interest which it may lawfully protect."[45] The majority disagreed. The same principle, however, may have been in the minds of some or most justices in many of the other cases which have been heard by the Court.[46]

It must be said that the difficulties of applying the test of clear and present danger to *subversive* activities are multiplied when it is applied to religious-liberty cases. For at least there is no doubt that the state may legally and morally protect itself against acts of subversion. But may it protect itself against disunity, or irreligious tendencies, or street littering, or invasion of the privacy of the home, or unauthorized parades, when these are relevant to the First Amendment? The question is not only whether the state can prevent such activities *at all*, but also whether the value of religious liberty is not higher than the other value concerned. In the Cox case the Court was not merely concerned with "maintaining public order without which liberty itself would be lost in the excesses of unrestrained abuses."[47] The real question was whether the holding of unauthorized parades constitutes such an excess, especially when the parade in question may be viewed as a religious exercise. The Court in the Cox case decided it was an excess; but it is clear that given a slightly different value hierarchy on the part of several judges, another conclusion might have been reached which would sound just as logical when enbalmed in judicial phraseology.

8. *Unavoidability of clash.* In Justice Murphy's hands the clear and present danger rule was easily turned into a doctrine that "a basic liberty can be limited only to the extent that the clash between its free exercise and the prevention of immediate substantive evil is unavoidable."[48] The use of such a doctrine would clearly have led to a different decision in the Cox and Prince cases.[49] It is in actuality only an extension of the clear and present danger rule by the addition of the test of inevitability of effect—a test which in some cases (though not in all) is no easier to apply. In the Jacobson compulsory vaccination case, for instance, to have based the decision on whether the lack of vaccination would have led "unavoidably" to a smallpox epidemic would have been literally impossible and unwise to the point of absurdity.[50]

But in some cases, like the Cantwell case, the test can seemingly be applied easily by merely looking at what happened. The state claimed that the actions of the Jehovah's Witnesses threatened the peace; but the Court overruled this contention because no actual breach of the peace had occurred. A clash was obviously not unavoidable if it had been avoided.[51] However, there is a difficulty in this: if the state were forced to wait until violations had occurred before it could act, its job of preventing such violations or breaches of the peace would be made impossibly difficult. Preventive action

is in many cases not only legitimate but necessary, a fact which
the unavoidability test fails to recognize. It has the value, however,
of emphasizing that proper watchfulness by the civil authorities, by
providing police protection or other means, might often prevent
any real threat of disorder, thus rendering unnecessary the deprivation
of freedom. American police authorities could learn a valuable lesson
from the London police in this respect.

5

The foregoing survey of the means by which a court can arrive
at a tenable decision in a case involving religious liberty emphasizes
the fact that no hard and fast rule of law can be applied. In spite
of the fulminations of critics, it is clear that the Court can only
proceed, in Justice Frankfurter's words, "from case to case."[52] It
is for this reason that the study of judicial decisions on religious
liberty becomes in reality not a study of law (not even "constitutional"
law) but an excursion into political philosophy. From our study of
the Court's philosophy it appears that the present justices almost
unanimously share the doctrines of Jefferson and Madison, and that
with these as a basis they add their own modern corollaries to fit
present-day problems and needs in accordance with the libertarian
spirit of those doctrines. Good grounds exist for the belief that the
Court in so acting is proceeding along the high road of liberty
blazed by Roger Williams and followed by the Revolutionary statesmen.

Whatever one's opinion as to that, however, it cannot be gainsaid
that for better or worse the Court has made a significant addition
to the theory of separation. It has set up the standard that no
American government can "pass laws which aid one religion, aid
all religions, or prefer one religion above another."[53] The "all
religions" clause has aroused a furore among many sincerely religious
people; it apparently results from the Court's feeling that any aid,
even ostensibly to "all" religions would (as in Champaign) in fact
aid one religion or prefer one religion over another. It is another
step in the long road toward state neutrality, and it is made necessary
at least in part by the existence of a huge group of citizens, probably
at least 45 per cent of the total, who are not religious and some

of whom are irreligious.[54] Such men and women have the same civil rights as the religious, and to tax or coerce them for the aid even of "all" religions would be as unfair as it was to tax Presbyterians for the support of Anglicanism.

In addition, the Court may pardonably suspect the sudden enthusiasms of some religious groups for aid to "all" religions, for it is at least possible that what these groups really want is aid to *their* religions. Is it not possible, in line with Madison's group theory explored earlier, that if the aid to all religions entailed aid to 16,000,000 Buddhists in the maintenance and propagation of their faith, this enthusiasm for religion in general would be revealed as an enthusiasm for, at most, Christianity in general? If the government can aid *all* religions, but is at the same time prevented from preferring one over another, this aid must extend to Buddhists in San Francisco, Jews in New York, and Bahais in Chicago, as well as to Presbyterians in Tennessee and Roman Catholics in Boston. It is understandable that neither the justices of the Supreme Court nor the various Christian churches are very eager to aid such non-Christian groups (or even some "fringe" Christian ones); but is it not more honest and honorable for the Court therefore to refuse to aid *any* religion than for the churches to speak of an aid to *all* religions to which they would almost surely object were not almost all American religions Christian? Would not these groups be the first to maintain complete separation (as did the Protestants when faced with Catholicism in the public schools) if they were faced with a dangerous threat from state-aided non-Christian religions? But since, as they see it, the major threat is non-*religious* in nature rather than non-*Christian*, they feel safe in asking for aid to "all religions."

So we find that after 350 years of struggle for religious liberty and the separation of church and state, vexing problems of the exact meaning of these concepts are still with us.[55] While they may not, as in earlier days, threaten the peace, order, and stability of the political society, they do endanger personal liberty and sometimes (as in antievolution or Bible-reading laws) infringe on academic freedom; they are therefore real and serious problems even today. On the solution to them depends the continuance of the American

99

march toward enlarged freedom, which is threatened in this sphere as in others. What are the possible and desirable solutions from the political point of view? That they may differ from those considered desirable from the religious viewpoint is possible and perhaps probable; at least, many sincere religious leaders believe so. The statesman and the political theorist, however, cannot be concerned with the fate of the church except in a subsidiary sense. The existence of a stable and free society is their aim. Conversely, church leaders are naturally concerned first of all with the welfare of the spiritual society, and the political is subsidiary with them.

My task is to proceed to an analysis of present-day problems from the political viewpoint; I leave to others the religious view. In our society, democratic as it is, the end result will probably be a compromise between the two. If such a compromise can be worked out, and if it stands the test of experience, providing freedom for both man and church, my aim will have been accomplished.

5

Contemporary American Problems

THE PRECEDING SURVEY of the history of the development of
the theory of separation has been undertaken with the aim
of providing a solid background for the construction of a
theory which can both be valid under present conditions and provide
answers for present problems. It is assumed that the understanding
of the present depends upon an understanding of the past; it is also
thought to be probable that some of the forces leading to separation
in the past may still be present today. Before we can proceed to the
construction of a theory, however, it is necessary that we have
some understanding of what the present-day conflicts between church
and state are. The present chapter is intended to provide this information.

The primary intention of this chapter and this book is not to
propose specific solutions for specific problems; the goal is merely
to build a framework within which attempts to solve problems
may proceed. Consequently, this chapter will attempt only to present
the problems and to analyze the relevant aspects of them, their
specific historical backgrounds, and in what ways they create tensions
between the religious and political spheres of human life. As stated
earlier, the principle of separation cannot eliminate conflict, but
it can perform the important task of minimizing it; therefore, even

though we have separation in the United States, this fact does not and cannot lead to the conclusion that there are no remaining problems. There probably will always be problems of church and state as long as men's allegiance is given both to a nation and to a God.

1

The development of the American public school system has been justified on two major counts: its necessity for the training of citizens for democratic action and its utility as a means of creating and maintaining a social unity among a diverse population. In both connections the existence of separate parochial school systems has raised problems.

Insofar as the schools are regarded as citizenship training agencies, the problem has not been of major proportions, apparently because it is commonly felt that there is no reason why private and parochial schools cannot accomplish this job as well as the public schools. Since the Supreme Court settled the legal question when Oregon attempted to abolish parochial schools, there has been little discussion or controversy regarding this aspect of the existence of these institutions.[1]* The present rapid growth of the parochial systems, and the possibility that the segregation problem will induce some Protestant churches to set up white schools, may increase the dimensions of the question in the future. However, it seems to be well accepted that the states have the right to require certain standards even of private schools as to teacher qualifications, curriculum, etc., most of which were set up at least partly because of the concern for citizenship training. Such laws it would seem, largely take care of the problem.

But the public schools also, it is often maintained, perform a valuable service in inculcating the social mores, creating in our population the social unity which is necessary to keep a culture viable and a political structure operating. This is done, so the arguments run, by breaking down the barriers of social class, of race, and of religious differences in the equalitarian atmosphere of the public school classroom.

* Notes to this chapter begin on page 166.

On the other hand, those who believe in the parochial system deny that religious schools have a markedly divisive influence; and in a more positive sense they go on to make the claim that the schools have a duty to educate the "whole man," which cannot be done, they say, without the inclusion of religious knowledge. Their conclusion is that the parochial school actually provides a *better* education, because it provides a more nearly complete one. It is such a philosophy of education which has led the Roman Catholic church not only to maintain but to expand its private school system.[2] There is, of course, a second motive of great importance: the training of the children of the church in the principles of its particular religion.

The general thesis of this author, which is presented in full in the following two chapters, is based on a theory of cultural pluralism and a belief in diversity. There are many pressures, both social and legal, in our society which lead toward at least a minimum cultural unity. The prevailing American middle-class morality affects us all regardless of what school we attend, for instance. There would seem to be room for great diversity in our educational system.

Further, it is not only true that any society needs a certain amount of shared assumptions and beliefs, but at the same time in the modern industrial world the danger really seems to be that there may be *too much* unity; that this unity may become a consciously nourished conformity rather than a voluntary sharing. I do not believe that parochial schools, even should they replace the public school system completely, would be the agents for the destruction of America. Nor, as should be plain from the argument which closes this book, is the religious school, privately financed and controlled, a violation of the principle of separation. Whether religion is a necessary part of a complete *formal* education is not a question particularly germane at this point, though it is of great significance in the next section.

2

A much more difficult issue to settle is that of the place, if any, of religion in the *public* schools. This is a question which has been before us ever since the first public schools were established; but with the growth of universal education, mostly in public schools, the question has become both more important and more difficult. The existence of the problem seems to be due to four major factors.

First, and perhaps most important in the contemporary scene, has been the relative failure of the churches, particularly the Protestant ones, to reach their youth successfully. This failure, although it cannot be documented quantitatively, seems to be a progressively expanding one in our secular society. With churchgoing, especially in Northern urban areas, becoming largely an adult and a once-a-week affair, the churches in the 1890's began to develop the modern Sunday School to educate their children in religious beliefs. Unfortunately the Sunday School has suffered from several difficulties in playing this role. Financially it has never been able to provide for professionally trained, paid teachers and effective teaching devices. As a matter of time, the one hour class a week definitely limits what could be done even with the best of personnel. But more significant, parents have refused to exercise firm parental pressure for regular attendance, and particularly has this been true of those who are not themselves regular churchgoers. The result has been that the Sunday Schools, on the whole, have reached only those children whose parents would probably have assumed some responsibility for their religious training in any case, and the churches have feared that they are failing to replenish their membership among the younger generations.[3]

From this standpoint it is obvious why church leaders may be interested in some kind of religious training in the public schools. With compulsory attendance such training would mean that the churches could reach practically every member of the grade and high school population, which means almost every American.

Second, as has been implied above, the religious philosophy of education is that education is incomplete without religious education. Modern public education attempts to reach the whole human being, to form his character and to shape his ideals as well as to give him knowledge. But how, it is asked, can this be done without religion being a part of education?[4]

Such an approach is abetted by the general trend in America for society to push off more and more of the wider educational process on the not necessarily unwilling schools. This trend implies that not only is education incomplete without religion, but also that it is the duty of the schools to provide *all* education, possibly not from the cradle to the grave, but certainly from five to seventeen. Within these ages Americans have more and more tended to assume that any training that is desirable should be given by the schools. Parents, church, and other organizations have practically abdicated their former educational roles. It has thus become almost true that if a child is to receive any training in ethics, morals, religion, art appreciation, or how to use a knife and fork, we depend on the schools to do it. That the schools have thus become overburdened to such an extent that they not only do these things badly, but also suffer in the performance of their more traditional duties, seems to have occurred to few religious leaders.

If there is danger of the growth of a monolithic state, that danger would not be averted by adding religious education to a public-school program which already embraces most fields of human thought. Quite the contrary, it would amount to handing over to the state almost the last bastion of knowledge which has been held inviolate.

Then too, it is possible that public-school religious education would in the long run be the type the state would permit, but not necessarily the kind the churches want. If society is secular in tone, the public schools will be; and any religion taught there is likely to be secular in nature. In any case "it is hardly lack of due process for the government to regulate that which it subsidizes."[5]

Third, there is an assumption precedent to that just surveyed. This is the assumption that society cannot exist without religion, or to put it more accurately, that American democratic society is a Christian form of polity and could not exist without Christianity. Churches and religious education are necessary, then, for the formation of the type of character needed in a democratic society.[6]

Fourth, it is felt by some religious leaders that the refusal of public schools to offer religious education is a denial of the freedom of religion, freedom being thus interpreted as the freedom to obtain religious knowledge at public expense, which is assumed to be a part of general religious liberty, whatever its connection with separation may be.[7]

The foregoing remarks are necessarily general and thus inaccurate.

Church schools are not always ineffective; all denominations do not abdicate their educational functions to the public schools; all public schools do not teach badly. But it is submitted, nevertheless, that the comments above are on the whole a fair summary of the reasons for the pressure for religious education given in, if not by, the public schools. The only significant exceptions fall into three categories: groups which, like the Catholics, have been able to maintain their own school systems and thus infiltrate the educational process with any religious content they like; groups which, like the orthodox Jews, have had the zeal and ingenuity to provide fairly adequate religious training *outside* school hours; and groups which in local areas are so predominant that they have been able to seize the public schools and use them to their own purposes, a situation which will be discussed briefly below.

Religious pressure on the schools has taken several forms and degrees. Most commonly it has been merely the demand that Bible reading, Bible stories, and the Lord's Prayer be made regular parts of the day's school work. Some states have been refused court assent to such programs, while others have been successful in getting approval or have avoided litigation challenging these arrangements.

The legal requirement of Bible reading seems to have spread rapidly in the twentieth century. Johnson and Yost in 1948 provided the following list of states, not necessarily complete, which have such laws. Bible reading is required in Alabama, Arkansas, Delaware, the District of Columbia, Florida, Georgia, Idaho, Kentucky, Maine, Massachusetts, New Jersey, Pennsylvania, and Tennessee. Further, some states *permit* Bible reading, optional either with teacher or with school board; Colorado, Indiana, Iowa, Kansas, Michigan, Minnesota, Mississippi, North Dakota, Ohio, Oklahoma, South Dakota, and Texas are the states which do so. Moreover, in some of these states children may not be excused from attendance at the Bible reading, although in some cases they may not be required to take part. Examples of such states are Alabama, Delaware, Florida, Kentucky, Maine, Massachusetts, and Pennsylvania.

At the same time there are a number of states in which Bible reading is not permitted, sometimes as state policy and sometimes because of court decision. Arizona, California, Illinois, Louisiana,

Nebraska, Nevada, New Mexico, New York, Utah, Washington, Wisconsin, and Wyoming were in this group as of 1948.[8]

The history of separation surveyed earlier if used a priori would lead one to believe that Bible reading and similar practices would be most likely to be required in states where there is the greatest religious homogeneity and prohibited in states with great religious diversity. While perhaps a tendency in this direction may be noted from the statistics given above, it certainly is not an invariable one. It is also true that in some states, such as New Mexico and Arizona, where there is a large Catholic population but where politics has traditionally been Protestant-controlled, the prohibition of Bible reading has had an anti-Catholic bias.

Various practical problems in the administration of such programs arise. Should those who do not wish to participate be excused? What version of the Bible can be agreed upon? Should teachers be allowed to comment on the readings? To answer questions? Can such a system be effectively policed so that teachers can do no proselyting? What about the religious beliefs of the teacher? Suppose he is a Jew or infidel; can he be forced to read the Bible? Such problems have led many school administrators to conclude that Bible reading, whatever its virtues, presents too many difficulties to be worth while.

It is not with such practical problems that this book is concerned, but rather with religious liberty and its maintenance. The question which arises in connection with Bible reading is this: How does it square with the principle of separation? No categorical answer will here be given; it is hoped that the use of the theory developed in Chapters 6 and 7 may provide a framework for such an answer. Here, however, some tentative considerations may be suggested.

If the state is, as Madison and Jefferson believed, incapable of judging the merits of any religious doctrine, the conclusion may be drawn that it cannot recognize any religion or even religion in general, since to do so would require just such a judgment. Even if the argument be accepted that social and political stability and morality are dependent upon a belief in religion, this argument may not lead to the conclusion that public-school religious teaching is needed. It is at least possible that those who want such teaching, beyond the mere Bible-reading stage, would be dissatisfied with it if they had it; for if the state were to teach religion, it would have to do so without regard to its truth or falsity.

If the schools had regular classes in religion, for instance, a measure which has recently been suggested in Florida, and which is to be tried in several selected schools during 1958-59, it would be necessary for them to teach not truth, of which the state cannot judge, but theory, with all sides weighed and open discussion urged. But a religious course taught with no presuppositions as to its truth, and taught only because of its supposed social utility, would not be very acceptable to the churches.

This point may be illustrated, at least as regards the university level, by comparing the teaching of theology with that of philosophy. In our university philosophy departments, provided they are good ones, many differing views are held or presented. There are Deweyites, neo-Thomists, Platonists, Marxists, Kantians, pragmatists, and many others. The student is thus exposed to many different versions of philosophical truth, any of which may be espoused, or at least presented, by particular professors. Ideally in each class free speculation exists. The student may embrace any philosophy which impresses him, or he may reject them all, either developing his own or deciding all philosophy is the "bunk."

The democratic school under separation may find that for both practical and theoretical reasons it must handle theological questions in the same way. It cannot force either its students or its teachers to espouse any particular theological viewpoint, but must allow all viewpoints to be presented, even though they may be non-Christian or nonreligious. The student would thus be free to accept any religious view, to combine them all, or to reject them all. But this, even were it otherwise acceptable to the churches, would not do the educational job which they claim needs to be done. It would not inculcate specifically Christian ethics, it would not necessarily increase church membership or appeal, and it certainly would not enhance the right of parents to have their children brought up in a particular faith.[9]

Even liberal theology rests on the acceptance of certain fundamentals, and consequently it is doubtful that many churches could accept the approach to religious education outlined above, especially if it were a required part of the schools' course work. In the theology of organized religion free speculation can proceed only within the limits of acceptance of the basis of theology itself, theism; and any particular denomination is likely to impose its own additional restrictions upon free thought. Catholics, for instance, would be unhappy with a religious training in the public schools which exposed the Holy Trinity or the virginity of Mary to speculation and doubt. As the nineteenth-century Catholic writer T. W. M. Marshall expressed it: "Now, as in all former ages, every speculation is legitimate, in every sphere of thought, subject to this sole restriction, that no conclusion can be admitted which contradicts a revealed truth previously established, and resting upon a fixed and immovable foundation."[10] This restriction differs only in detail from the necessary conditions imposed by any religious organization, or indeed by any voluntary association of any type. One may be a citizen without accepting the political philosophy on which the state rests, since the state is a compulsory organization from which he cannot withdraw or easily be expelled (though his political rights may be withdrawn). But the very existence of a voluntary organization depends on belief in it (or at least tacit acceptance) by all its members; and indeed, such belief is the only proper reason for membership. The labor union cannot admit members who do not believe in labor unions unless perchance they are willing to keep quiet about it. No more can a church admit members who do not accept its basic dogmas, for as Winthrop Hudson points out, "If it imposes no tests for membership and makes no provision for discipline, it will not only display no distinctive quality of life but in due time will have nothing to say except that which everyone will be saying."[11]

Religious education from the standpoint of the organized religious denomination, therefore, cannot be anything but the inculcation of belief. It is reasonable to suppose that such inculcation is actually what the churches are asking for; but it also seems clear that this is just what the state cannot consent to do. Nothing said herein should be interpreted as meaning that religious training is not necessary or desirable; the question is, who is to give it?

The final plea of some churchmen that lack of religious education in the public schools is a denial of the religious liberty guaranteed by the Constitution is open to serious question. It is true, no doubt, that the democratic state cannot deprive any person of the freedom to receive religious instruction; it does not necessarily follow that such education should be given by the state at public expense. The fact that a child does not receive such training in the public school does not deprive him of his freedom to receive it at all! The churches remain open, and parents are free to send their children to them for religious instruction either in the form of church-school on Sunday, of week-day classes, or of complete educational systems. If the appeal of the church is not great enough to attract students to such programs, the fault is the church's, not the state's; nor is it the duty of the state to make up for the delinquencies of the church in this regard. Indeed it would seem that the state has gone quite far enough in its Sunday legislation which sets aside that day from normal school activities, leaving it open for such schooling as the churches are willing and able to provide.

3

More serious than Bible reading in terms of its impact upon school programming and on the effectiveness of religious training in recent years has been the development of "released-time" and "dismissed-time" programs.[12] Although there are many variations in these programs, they ordinarily operate in somewhat the following manner. "Released-time" involves the setting up of religious classes inside the school and during school time, but ordinarily taught by representatives of religious groups. This is the arrangement that the Supreme Court found unconstitutional in the McCollum case. For the religious group such a program has important advantages: it permits at least one period a week of religious training in the coercive atmosphere of the public school day and school building. Thus it reaches a maximum number of children for the same length of time as the Sunday School. Because the time can be staggered for different schools or different grades, the larger religious denominations can afford to hire professional teachers or ministers who can make the most of the time permitted.

At the same time there are defects from the religious standpoint.

Such a program involves state favoritism, in effect, toward those religious groups which are numerically large or wealthy, since they have the resources to provide programs, and good ones, and enough students to make it worth while. For this reason many of the smaller sects have opposed released time, at least in areas where they are numerically too weak to participate. Jews have objected because they are relatively well satisfied with their Saturday schools. Atheists and agnostics object because their children are sometimes subjected to social coercion and ridicule if they do not participate.

"Dismissed-time" programs avoid some of these defects by giving up the advantages. The children are dismissed from school perhaps an hour early once a week on securing their parents' and their own pledges that they will proceed from school to their church for an hour of religious instruction. This idea has resulted in much lower participation by children; since attendance cannot be compelled by state law (probably), many children leave school but never arrive at church; many parents will not sign such pledges; and of course it is difficult to figure out what to do with the children who remain at school. If they are left free to play or do as they please, the religious program seems unattractive by comparison; but on the other hand, if they are given serious work to do they may progress more rapidly in school work than their churchgoing comrades. The distance of the various churches from the school also appears to be a limiting factor in many cases.

Both released- and dismissed-time plans are open to the objection that they divide children into groups on a basis unrelated to strictly educational objectives and may foster bad feeling in the student body of the school. Such charges are, however, largely undocumented, and it is difficult to figure out how much of them is conjecture.

The Supreme Court of the United States has decided that released time is unconstitutional but dismissed time is not, basing its decisions on its interpretation of the Jeffersonian theory of separation outlined in Chapter 3.[13] If the Protestant churches were strong enough to do as the Catholics and Jews have done, much of the desire for dismissed- or released-time programs would probably disappear, but for various reasons the Protestant churches do not feel that after-school or Saturday religious classes would be successful.

111

4

Although the public schools are theoretically controlled by the entire community, there have been a few cases in which they have fallen under the actual control of a denominational group. Such instances have generally been of one of two types.[14] In one type an entire school system in a county or town may be controlled by a denomination which is so strong in that area that almost all the students, teachers, and school-board members are of that group. In the other type, more usual in larger centers of population, a parochial school may be taken into the public school system even though the school continues to be run by the church.

In certain areas of New Mexico and Arizona which are populated largely by Mexicans and Indians almost 100 per cent of the people are Catholic. In such places the public schools have often taken on quite a pronounced Catholic flavor, and in fact the Catholic church in the past did not bother to maintain parochial schools in these areas, for it was able to arrange the curriculum to suit itself, to use nuns in full regalia as teachers, and in general to obtain the same benefits as from parochial schools without the expense involved. The same thing happened when the Indian schools were transferred from Catholic hands to the federal government early in the twentieth century. While such occurrences have not been frequent, they have come up often enough, and have been scattered around the country in such a way as, to lend substance to the fear that they would be more common if other religious groups relaxed their vigilance.

The other type of church control of public schools may be illustrated graphically by the famous College Hill controversy. North College Hill is a suburb of Cincinnati; in 1940 for two years, and again in 1946, the Grace Avenue Parochial School was rented from the Catholic church by the school board, which then paid the salaries of the eight nuns who taught there. Religious garb was worn by the teachers, Catholic symbols decorated the building, and Catholic instruction was a part of the regular courses. The arrangement when it became publicly known caused great bitterness and controversy between Catholic and non-Catholic groups in the community and forced the resignation of the entire school board. It was claimed at the time that over 350 parochial schools in the United States were being so supported.

From the religious viewpoint such arrangements are generally entered into for financial reasons, though it is also true that the Catholic church in particular has no doctrinal opposition to state support. However, even many Catholic officials have objected to them, for they fear that state support will lead eventually to state control. Probably the chief practical difficulty, however, is the fact that such sectarian control of a public school or a public school system is likely to lead to religious controversy and bring religion into politics in ways that may disrupt community life; in other words, it may cause exactly the type of religion-based struggle which the separation of church and state was designed to avert. Neighbor becomes aligned against neighbor in a way that could not happen ordinarily in this country, for ordinarily religious and political differences are not combined. Thus, as Johnson and Yost remark, the result of such attempts by churches to obtain public support for their own schools is "dissension," "neighborhood bitterness," and "educational chaos."[15]

While it is less important, the problem of the wearing of religious costume by teachers in public schools has also arisen as an issue, and the courts in such instances have almost always ruled against the practice. On a lesser scale it may cause the same untoward results as actual religious control.

5

A relatively new problem in church-state relations, still within the area of education, has been presented by the development in many school systems of the practice of providing various services to the students, such as dental and physical examinations, free textbooks, police protection at crossings, school bus or paid public transportation, or (possibly) the payment of tuition to parochial schools.[16] The question involved, of course, is whether such benefits should be provided to all school children regardless of the school they attend or only to public-school children. The United States Supreme Court ruled on such a question when it upheld the provision of bus fare by the state to all children regardless of the school attended.[17]

The rationale of such aid is obvious: the aid is to the child, not to the school, and thus should be given to all children on an equal basis. This is true, however, only under certain circumstances which the churches might not approve. In the case of textbooks, for instance, even though one were to concede that state funds could be expended to supply children with books, this would clearly be true only if the books were completely nonreligious. If the parochial schools chose texts written by Catholic authors for Catholic children, the state money would obviously be aiding the religion, not merely the children. Of course there is also a tangential sense in which any aid to the children also aids the school, since it either reduces the finances necessary to run the school or makes the school more attractive to parents than it might otherwise be.

Consequent to these arguments for and against such aid, there has been much controversy and litigation on the wisdom and the constitutionality of such aid to parochial school children. It thus qualifies as another of the problems with which any theory of separation of church and state must cope.

6

Often in the modern world, due to factors which we have already surveyed, men are faced with the difficult choice of whether to obey the dictates of church and conscience or the orders of the state. In the ancient world such conflicts were rare; then religion was civic religion, for the most part bound up with the whole fabric of community life in a way that is unthinkable today. Two areas of such conflict have been particularly prominent in the United States in recent years: the problem posed by the demands of patriotism and national unity and that posed by the police power, the maintenance of public order. Both problems have been presented to us largely because of the rise in the nation of a truly "old-time" religion, the Jehovah's Witnesses. The Jehovah's Witnesses are "old-time" in several senses, including their fundamentalism; but what is primarily of interest here is that they represent a throwback to the early days of sectarianism; they are in many ways similar to the early Quakers, Baptists, and Methodists.

Sociologically there seems to be a rather normal pattern for religious groups which may be summarized by saying that they tend to start as sects and evolve into churches. As new groups they are rebels against existing religious patterns (although not necessarily in matters of dogma). They believe in a seven-day-a-week religion; they proselyte actively and have no objection to "stealing" members from other groups; they use lay and itinerant preachers; in general they have a zeal and enthusiasm which are embarrassing to partisans of older groups. However, as the sect becomes large, wealthy, and firmly established, it begins more and more to conform to the typical church pattern: a formal, more or less ritualized Sunday service; a *modus vivendi* with other denominations as to proselyting; an established ordained clergy trained for the ministry; and among its members an indistinguishability from members of other groups.[18]

It is natural that a denomination which has already completed this transition dislikes sects which are just starting out. Partly this is mere social snobbery, partly it is fear, partly it is dislike of "excessive" religious enthusiasm. But in addition to the fact that the older groups dislike the zealous sect, our modern secular life-conditions also cause a good deal of objection to the enthusiasm of the sectarian: we tend to regard it as obnoxious, embarrassing, and in general objectionable. So, from both the churches and individuals the government is pressured to act to prevent sectarian partisans from pursuing their activities.

In colonial times, as we have seen, the "established" Congregationalists and Anglicans used such methods against the lay riders and zealous missionary activities of the Baptists, the Presbyterians, the Quakers, and the Methodists. But 200 years have passed, and the once-sectarian groups have become churches. They oppose the present-day practices of the Jehovah's Witnesses—the principal modern "sect"—in the same ways and for the same reasons they themselves were opposed earlier.

The consequence in the United States has been the enactment of a whole host of municipal ordinances and state laws which, while often framed in general terms, are aimed at the "unusual" religious practices of the Jehovah's Witnesses. Street-littering laws have been passed to prevent the passing out of pamphlets; parade-licensing acts, to prevent street processions; antinoise statutes, to prevent the use of loud-speakers; booksellers-licensing laws, to prevent sale of propaganda literature; "privacy of the home" legislation, to prevent door-to-door religious canvassing; and other types of legislation. Being a contentious sect, the Jehovah's Witnesses have contested such actions by holding unauthorized parades and by refusing to pay special license taxes or to apply for permits, basing such refusal on their rights to conduct themselves as their religion requires. While such litigation as has resulted has been, of course, based on constitutional aspects of separation rather than on the theory itself, there is involved rather obviously the application of the theory of separation. To what extent general laws passed under the police power or the power to promote national unity should be applicable to religious adherents who object to obedience because of their religion has been discussed in the preceding chapter in constitutional terms.

7

The rise of the modern national state which demands the primary allegiance of its citizens has posed serious questions for the religious citizen. At what point may the demands of the state in terms of loyalty and patriotism be set aside by the religious conscience? Or is there any such point? Is religious freedom actually to obtain only in such areas as the state in its wisdom sees fit to allow? When the state demands action "for the good of the state" or for "national security," does such claim foreclose the issue?

Such questions are typical in the modern age. Perhaps the most famous instances in the United States have revolved around attempts to maintain national defense and to inculcate national unity. The development of the civilian army—the draft and universal military service—beginning with the Civil War has meant that those individuals who believe their religion commands them not to fight have been placed in the position of having to refuse obedience either to conscience or to government. Modern nationalism causes the conscientious objector to be popularly regarded as a coward or even a traitor; with such feelings we have here no direct concern. More basic is the question whether the individual has the right to refuse to serve in the armed forces, and whether the state has a right to compel him to do so or to punish him for not doing so.

Possibly the most likely answer is that, in line with the theory presented in this study, each individual must decide for himself whether he is to abide by the claims of conscience or those of government. But at the same time the government cannot allow citizens to decide for themselves when to obey the laws and when not to; therefore the government must have the right to deal with disobedience, under the law, as it sees fit. Such an answer, it is obvious, places a great deal of reliance on the good sense and the restraint of government officials and of the general public. On the whole, United States history as to conscientious objectors seems to indicate that this reliance has not been misplaced; but with nationalism more rampant than ever, even to the point of chauvinism, one may well wonder whether the future will deal so tenderly with objectors "for cause of conscience."

A second question which has arisen in this country has grown out of the increased pressures for unity and conformity during the Second World War and the cold war following it. Many states or their local school officials have required the administration of the salute to the flag for all school children each day. But some religious groups—Jehovah's Witnesses, Mennonites, and others—regard the flag salutes as obeisance to idols or as placing worship of nation before that of God. Such groups have often instructed their children to refuse to salute the flag. The recent addition to the flag salute of the phrase "under God" has perhaps lessened the objections of some religionists, but it has at the same time made the flag salute impossible for agnostics or atheists honorably to take. Consequently we find nowadays opposition to the flag salute coming from three sources: those who feel it is a violation of their religion, those who grant no allegiance to any god, and those who do not believe the state should require any religious test or oath.[19]

Such a situation places school officials in a quandary. For assuming that the flag salute is a valid and valuable means of inculcating patriotism and unity, such effect would be largely vitiated if anyone who wishes may refuse to take it. Yet to force all to take it may violate the principles of religious liberty and separation of church and state! Parents, too, have serious problems. School attendance is compulsory; if the school requires the flag salute, children may be expelled for failing to take it. Then the parents may be indicted in court for contributing to truancy. On the other hand, as is sometimes the case, parents and child may be in fear lest they "incur the righteous wrath" of God by taking the salute!

Such conflicts of conscience are endemic to a system of separation of church and state. They are, however, *epidemic* where the state has legal control of religion. Our question is how such problems may be met under the theory of separation with due regard both for the requirements of nationalism and security and for those of religious liberty.

8

In two instances the incompatibility of separation and state action is so obvious that it is not necessary to withhold judgment. Blasphemy laws present a rather obvious case of the protection of religion by the state. It is fairly clear that the irreligious person or the non-Christian cannot logically blaspheme Christianity. For blasphemy can only be defined in reference to the religion which is blasphemed. Consequently, from the personal standpoint it is impossible to blaspheme something in which one does not oneself believe. An atheist cannot blaspheme a god in whom he does not believe; a Muslim cannot blaspheme the Christian Trinity; and non-Catholics cannot blaspheme the Virgin Mary. If the state is religiously neutral, as the principle of separation assumes, there can be no such thing as blasphemy from the political viewpoint, for to pass and enforce a blasphemy law would be for the political to take sides on a religious question. A more obvious violation of the separation principle is difficult to imagine.

It is true, however, that many states have blasphemy laws on the books today. Such laws are relics of colonial religious attitudes, and are seldom enforced any longer. What we used to regard as blasphemy and to make illegal is in reality poor taste and poor manners, and it should be treated as such rather than as a breach of the law.

Some years ago, particularly in the colonies before the American Revolution, but later also in some of the states, there were laws requiring witnesses in court to take an oath on the Bible, or to believe in a future state of rewards and punishments, or something similar. Such laws were the result of the belief that non-Christians or atheists could not be credible witnesses. Here, too, the secular state cannot require such qualifications of a witness without clearly violating the separation principle. The state cannot officially place all beliefs on an equal plane and yet by this method deny that an atheist or a Confucianist can be as good a citizen as can a Christian. The state must judge men by their acts, not by their beliefs.

It may be added that the efficacy of religious tests is extremely doubtful, as all the leading thinkers on toleration have seen. An unbeliever may be willing to swear on the Bible or any other book; the fact that he does so hardly makes him a more credible witness than he would be if he refused to do so.

9

Several other typical problems which arise under a system of separation of church and state may be briefly mentioned. The brevity is justified by the fact that these practices, whatever their theoretical status, are well accepted as legitimate concessions by the state.

The so-called "Sunday legislation" by which Sunday is made a legal holiday and some businesses are forbidden to operate goes back into ancient times. It is in origin a token of respect to the Christian Sabbath granted by the state. Nevertheless, its wisdom is seldom questioned today. We usually take for granted the desirability of having one day of rest a week, and the fact that it happens to come on the Christian Sabbath may be regarded as merely a convenience.[20]

Tax exemption is a subsidy granted by the state to religious institutions. Yet at the same time taxation can so obviously be used to discriminate or prohibit that there is little real question that exemption is a desirable practice. What cannot be achieved by direct legislation can often be achieved through the taxing power; and regardless of theoretical principles, the separation of church and state may be partially dependent on the preservation of the tax exempt status of religion.

From the religious standpoint one may perhaps question the morality of the churches in accepting tax exemption. A church which depends on such indirect subsidies may not be morally free to criticize the subsidizing agent. But subsidies are such a pervasive feature of modern government that such a consideration loses much of its force. Practically all groups in modern society are subsidized in one way or another, and their right to criticize is not thereby given up. Practically speaking, then, tax exemption may at least be considered a wise governmental policy, consistent with the *operation* of separation if not strictly with its theory.[21]

Chaplainships present somewhat similar questions. We have seen that James Madison objected to the hiring of chaplains by the government, and a few states, notably Michigan, constitutionally forbid the employment of a chaplain for the legislature. One may regard such chaplainships as a recognition merely of the fact that most members of the legislature are Christians rather than as a governmental recognition of religion as such, and in any case the duties of legislative chaplains are so light that few worry about the compatibility of the situation with the separation principle.

Somewhat more serious considerations are involved, however, when one turns to the armed-forces chaplainships. While the state is merely recognizing the religious proclivities of its soldiery in offering them religious services on a voluntary basis, the church does face a moral ambiguity. It has been said that the presence of chaplains constitutes a renunciation of the church's announced objective of world peace, substituting a tacit sanction of war; this is particularly so since the chaplains are state employees and members of the armed forces.[22] Where then does the chaplain's primary loyalty lie: to the church and the faith which he represents or to the state and the military arm in which he serves? He may be, as one writer has pointed out, "so completely at home in the military atmosphere that he is not as sensitive to the unchristian character of the whole psychology of preparedness for war and justification of war as a

Christian minister ought to be."[23] Further, even if the chaplain
retains his moral sensitivity, he may lose much of his freedom to
express it. "He is often unable to exercise an attitude of ethical
criticism toward issues of war and peace, and if he should do so
he would find himself in such sharp conflict with his military superiors
that from their point of view he could no longer be an acceptable
chaplain."[24]

Yet it may be admitted that the church's own point of view forbids
the desertion of its own adherents in the armed forces, either in
war or peace. Perhaps the only solution—a partial one at best—
would be for the churches themselves to employ the chaplains, who
could then be merely attached to the military, as newspaper corre-
spondents often are. The military authorities would be no happier
about clerical criticism, but the clerics would at least not be directly
disloyal to their own employers and would be ethically free to
disregard such displeasure.[25]

10

A final grave and difficult problem remains to be mentioned. This
is the question of the right of the churches to press for morals
legislation in line with the requirements of their religious creeds.
The desirability, if not the rightness, of such action was brought
into serious question by the success of certain religious groups in
securing the passage of the prohibition amendment and the subsequent failure of the amendment to work.

Possibly the most important point to be made in this connection
is that there are various types of political action. If there is a
principle of separation of church and state in operation, it must
at least bar two types of political action: a direct role of the church
in government and a church-sponsored political party. There are
two other types of political activity permissible in a democracy,
both of which can be used by religion. These are the pressure group,
which a church organization may from the political standpoint
legitimately be, and the action of individual church members acting
on the basis of their own religious convictions.

It must be emphasized, however, that when the church speaks on political questions, it speaks as a pressure group among many pressure groups, not as an infallible expositor of the good. Its prescriptions must be judged from the standpoint of their political wisdom and feasibility, not on the basis of their creedal orthodoxy or command. Equally, when the Christian individual acts in politics, he acts as a citizen, not as a Christian.

Thus it would seem that prohibition could well be pushed by Christians and by churches, not, however, because it is a Christian moral principle, but because it may be argued as a social necessity or a social good. On the other hand, it would seem wrong for the religious citizen to press for antievolution laws, for no justification for these exists except in terms of the religious principles of particular groups. The question of political activities by churches is discussed at somewhat greater length in Chapter 7.

11

The foregoing survey of existing problems in the area of church-state relations was intended to illustrate two things: first, that the existence of a principle of separation of church and state does not automatically prevent all conflicts and problems between the two institutions; and second, that there are existing today grave problems with which any theory of separation must deal. With this survey— brief and necessarily incomplete as it is—it is possible to continue to the formulation of a theory of separation which will be relevant to actual conditions in the United States today.

6

Possible Church-State Relationships

E WHO READS AND THINKS even briefly about the problems of church and state will readily perceive that there are several possible relationships between these two enduring social institutions. These relationships may be separated into eight broad classifications; it should, however, be borne in mind that such groupings, put down on paper, seem more distinct than they ever are in human history. There are ideal-typical theoretical possibilities of each of the eight, but historical situations are difficult to classify into such neat compartments; the eight classifications grade off into each other in an infinite number of actual and potential realities. Still, there is value in the realization that these pure theoretical concepts exist, and it is probable that as ideas they have greatly influenced actuality in the Western world since before the Christian era.

1

Our study of the historical background of the church-state problem as it exists in the United States today is important in thinking about these classifications. This is true because the present situation grows out of the events and ideas of the past—the classical and medieval background which is the common heritage of all Western civilization, plus the specifically Anglo-American heritage which led to significant changes from the European pattern of church-state relationships. The American doctrine of separation of church and state is a striking illustration of these changes, for it is a doctrine and a practice that is unique. Its uniqueness and its practicality make it a worthy object of study. I would be the first to disclaim any suggestion that separation can be applied with equal effectiveness in all times and in all places, for it is the outgrowth of the thought and experience of a particular people and a particular age. Therefore, while separation on the American pattern may not be feasible everywhere, it follows also that other resolutions of the conflict between God and Caesar may not be feasible here. This statement calls for another disclaimer: separation as we know it was not inevitable. It is the product of innumerable choices made at innumerable times. It is inevitable only in the sense that our steps cannot be retraced.

Neither is its future inevitable; there are before us an almost unlimited number of alternative paths. Yet it should be obvious that in a relative sense these alternatives are few because there are so many possible ones which have been discarded in the past and have been rendered impossible by the march of history. This is only to say that at any particular point in history our range of choice is limited by the choices we have made previously, but that at the same time an extremely wide range yet remains in which choices must still be made.[1]*

Following are the eight broad classifications of church-state relationships: Pure Theocracy, Total Separation, Mixed Theocracy, Total Identification, Total Conflict, Erastianism, Totalitarianism, and Partial Separation. The last of these is the American solution; it is further discussed in Chapter 7.

The first two have never been attained in the modern world, and the second may be impossible except in pure theory. For these reasons they seem to be outside the range of possibility for the United States in the foreseeable future. I believe totalitarianism may be similarly discarded, at least for the present, since it has never

* Notes to this chapter begin on page 167.

yet been approached in the Anglo-Saxon countries. All except total separation have been actualities in one degree or another in Western history.

Philosophically as distinct from practically, however, all eight are worthy of consideration, since what is philosophically desirable does not depend on whether it is socially practicable. For this reason some attention will be given to all, reserving major consideration for those which are more nearly possible of attainment.

2

Pure theocracy may be defined as a situation in which the actual political authority is held and exercised by the heads of the ecclesiastical organization. The implications are that in such a condition the state as a political institution would not exist because the church would perform all the political functions.

Such a situation is about as fantastic a dream as could be imagined in the modern world, whatever its chances may have been in medieval days. The only approximation to it in Christian history would be the Papal States of Italy in the medieval and early modern period. Of these states the Pope was the political head, very much engaged not only in domestic but in international politics. It has been written that "Not only was the administration of the State absolutely unchecked by popular representation and a public press, but it was entirely in the hands of a class, or rather caste, of ignorant and bigoted ecclesiastics."[2]

Whatever may be one's view of the quality of priestly rule, it seems obvious that conditions in our days make such an idea illusory. For it depends, first of all, upon a religious uniformity and strength that cannot be found in the world today, not even in states which are both religiously homogeneous and strong in piety. Religion is no longer the force it once was.

It also seems to be true that even in the heyday of the medieval papacy no one ever seriously considered doing away with the secular political organization. Even Aegidius Romanus, the high priest of papal supremacy, did not go this far. Therefore the alternative of pure theocracy need not be considered seriously.

125

3

The nature of government and of religion, and particularly of the Christian religion, make total separation a purely theoretical idea. No state has ever achieved it, nor will any. Yet the idea of total separation has a certain significance, both because it brings out a particular concept of what religion is or should be and because some of the leading writers on the subject have perceived only dimly the impossibility of its achievement.

Total separation assumes that religion is subjective and pietistic, but this view of religion is not typical of the Western World and certainly not of Christianity. There are, it is true, certain Christian sects which have approached this ideal, particularly some of the German pietistic sects and, at times, the Quakers. Christianity as a whole, however, has always attempted through the church organization to guide man's actions as well as his soul; for this reason it has inevitably come into conflict with the state, which also must concern itself with the overt expressions of human life. The subjective ideal of religion which might produce total separation would at the same time restrict the influence of organized religion to so small an area of human activity that it would cease to be a real force in human society.[3]

It is this fallacious concept of what religion is in our civilization that led Williams, Locke, and Jefferson perilously close to the espousal of total separation. It is only in such a belief that Locke could write that "if each of them would contain itself within its own bounds—the one attending to the worldly welfare of the common-wealth, the other to the salvation of souls—it is impossible that any discord should ever have happened between them."[4] The whole argument of Roger Williams implies the same conviction; especially in his comparisons of the state and the church to a ship's crew and passengers does he seem to say that if only each would confine itself to its own sphere, peace would reign supreme.[5] Finally, Jefferson in his wall-of-separation metaphor is implicitly asserting a similar belief.[6]

Yet it must be granted that each of the trio saw, even if imperfectly, that what they were asking was impossible, that some conflicts were bound to occur even with the most rigid separation. They each admitted that the practice of some religious tenets might interfere with the peace and order of society. It is significant that all three, even the personally fanatical Williams, gave the same answer to the problem posed by such a conflict: that the state must impose its standard. Williams, for instance, when faced with problems of religious license in Rhode Island, invariably drew the line where disturbance of the civil peace began. The Rhode Island charter granted complete religious freedom, subject, however, to the qualification that citizens must behave themselves "peacablie and quietlie" without causing "lycentiousnesse and profanesse" or "civill injurye or outward disturbance of others."[7]

Similarly, Locke's refusal to tolerate Catholics and atheists was an implicit recognition, and a very important one, that religion and politics may and do conflict. He could not envisage a separation so far-reaching as to permit the practice of such beliefs, which he believed were subversive of state and society. His comments on animal sacrifices also recognize the possibility of conflict, and here he explicitly gives the power of decision to the state:

But if peradventure such were the state of things that the interest of the commonwealth required all slaughter of beasts should be forborne for some while . . . who sees not that the magistrate, in such a case, may forbid all his subjects to kill any calves for any use whatsoever? . . . But those things that are prejudicial to the commonweal of a people in their ordinary use, and are therefore forbidden by laws, those things ought not to be permitted to Churches in their sacred rites.[8]

Finally, Jefferson in his "wall of separation" letter ended by averring that the civil authorities could interfere if the civil peace was disturbed, if, as he puts it, the religious practices "break out into overt acts against peace and good order."[9]

Thus we see that even the most uncompromising advocates of separation of church and state have realized, perhaps unconsciously, that *total* separation in the sense of absolute elimination of the possibility of conflict was impossible, however desirable they may have thought it. Whether or not it would be possible in the non-Christian east where quietistic religions exist is a question which need not concern us.

4

In mixed theocracy the state is regarded as subordinate to the church even in temporal affairs. It is allowed only such autonomy as the church is willing to grant it. Generally, the state is regarded as the enforcement agency for the church; in medieval terminology, the wielder of the sword. This is a doctrine that has been espoused by many theorists and practiced in some degrees by some states.

In essence, Aegidius Romanus and Pope Boniface VIII desired a mixed theocracy in which the pope was to be the supreme arbiter of Christendom with the power to depose kings, to judge certain civil causes, and in general to define his own jurisdiction and that of the civil magistrate.[10] The state was to be the coercive arm of the church, to suppress heresy and also to maintain religious unity, although this second aspect of the religious claim was not too obvious before the Reformation brought a real threat to that unity. After the Reformation the maintenance of the "true faith" in the community became a very serious problem which confronted both the reformers and the Catholic hierarchy. Varying solutions were found; but John Calvin, most of all, advanced the doctrine of mixed theocracy and enforced it in Geneva in his lifetime.

Calvin regarded the religious community as standing above the civil state, which existed for him principally as an agency to enforce the Calvinistic discipline; the Genevan state was constructed with this in mind. The ministers, led by Calvin himself, controlled the political machinery, which was used to maintain rigorous regulations and included regular visitations by the authorities to the homes of the populace in order to ascertain that they obeyed these rules. Calvin's doctrines were taken up by John Knox in Scotland and extended to include active resistance to a religiously erring ruler and even tyrannicide—an idea which produced a reaction by James VI (later James I of England) in the direction of divine right.

A partial application of mixed theocracy existed in the early Massachusetts Bay Colony. It did not fit neatly into this category, but certain elements in its genesis and growth indicated a distinct tendency toward theocracy. It was above all a religious colony, formed by one religious group for a specifically religious purpose.

In each new town, as it was established, the founders first formed themselves into an ecclesiastical polity, and only then into a civil establishment. The governor and the assistants, all the members of the General Court, and even all the enfranchised citizens, were required to be members of the Congregational church. In a very real sense, therefore, Massachusetts was not a state with a church but a church with a state.

But the spirit of the seventeenth century ran against such systems of control and has done so ever more strongly up to the present day. Increasing secularization, the influx of dissenting groups, and the fragmenting tendencies apparent in Protestantism everywhere have prevented such a setup from achieving any sort of permanence. In spite of the Puritan heritage of the American people, there is no likelihood that any sort of mixed theocracy is possible in the United States today. Our counter-heritage of rationalistic thought, freedom, and political constitutionalism, plus religious divisions and the general decline of religious influence, seem to indicate that the nation has left irrevocably behind any such strict religious discipline.

5

Another possible relationship is total identification of church and state, an arrangement which is in some degree merely a variant form of mixed theocracy. Total identification assumes that the church and the state are coextensive geographically and that every citizen—in fact every resident—is subject, not only to the state politically, but also to the national church. It also assumes a complete identity of viewpoint between political authorities and the ecclesiastical hierarchy, the only condition which could assure the complete cooperation of both and the satisfaction of each with the existing relationship. It is difficult to see how such a condition could possibly last for any length of time; sooner or later it would seem that inevitable differences of viewpoint must be bred by the differences of function. Inexorably one side or the other would be drawn to seek supremacy rather than mere equality—if only, in its own view, to protect its own equality!

The conditions of total identification were most nearly met, in our history, in Massachusetts Bay, where for some thirty years what was extremely close to an identity of viewpoint existed between the Puritan church and state. This was largely due to the unique circumstances under which the colony was born, and it could be maintained only so long as the population remained religiously homogeneous and the religion retained its early fervor and strength. Neither condition could be long maintained; ultimately the political interests of the state, the religious divisions of the church, and the decline of religion as a force in men's lives led to an incompatibility which made a divorce a necessity.

Such identity as existed in New England rested on no formalized structure, since it was based on similarity of point of view rather than structural arrangement. In this sense it may even be said that the United States in the nineteenth century belonged in this classification. Some commentators have always insisted that this is a Christian nation, even in the legal sense.[11] In the social sense we have certainly shown the earmarks of being one. All during the last century businessmen and those desiring social advancement found it advisable to be Christians. It was sometimes difficult for non-Christians to obtain employment, and even though no religious test could be imposed on political officeholders, it was well for a presidential aspirant to be a Protestant.[12] Much of this is still the case.

This has resulted in legislation that lawmakers can characterize as being "in the Christian spirit." It has also meant that the strongly organized churches have a political strength which is often not accounted for by their numbers nor responsible to their members, as was illustrated in the prohibition drive and in the antievolution drive which received great publicity due to the Scopes trial. The effective movie censorship which restricts movie producers in the types of films they produce, under pressure from the Catholic church, is another case in point.[13]

It is true that this analogy cannot be carried very far. Although the United States may be in one sense a Christian nation, in another sense it is and has been one of the most strongly secular nations of the Western World, a fact which is illustrated by American leadership in the development of the separation doctrine. Another indication is the constant and continuing secularization of education. In the present day any identification of religion and politics seems

130

anachronistic. In a nation almost half of whose citizens are not members of any church; in which at least half of the church members are so only in name; in which the courts can reject released-time religious education as unconstitutional; in which millions of non-Christian religionists reside, practice their own religions, and exercise the same civil rights as Christians—in such a nation any real identity between the religious and the political points of view must be either coincidental or a result of political pressure rather than voluntary agreement.

6

The relation of total conflict between church and state in its fullest meaning is a relatively recent development. It is only recently that any Western state has been frankly antireligious or even anti-Christian. But in the modern totalitarian state, as exemplified in both Nazi Germany and Soviet Russia there is a genuine attempt on the part of the state to take over complete control of human life and activity; this is a tendency which, moreover, exists to a lesser degree even in modern democracies as a logical result of the industrialization and urbanization of twentieth-century life.

A totalitarian state is bound to come into conflict with any other social association which has any claims to independent control over the citizen. The problem is complicated when such a state is confronted by a religious group which also claims to be supreme in all the moral problems with which mankind is faced. Such a view is typical of the Christian churches, and particularly of Roman Catholicism. In this situation conflict rages throughout the area of human life. It is truly a total conflict in the ideological field. This it is which has forced the Catholic church, ordinarily rather indifferent to forms of government, to oppose Nazism and Communism, and which drove even some German Lutherans, despite their belief in passive obedience, into active opposition to Hitlerism.

It seems, however, that total conflict can be only temporary, for in any conflict there is (discarding the possibility of a compromise, which in view of totalitarian claims by both sides is unlikely) a victor and a vanquished. The conflict must end in the supremacy of one claim and possibly in the extinction of the other. Total conflict is also theoretically impermanent; it is a condition that neither side can accept, even in theory, since acceptance of it involves, or is believed to involve, the admission that there is some validity to the claims of the other side.

7

The Erastian solution to the problem of church and state is one seen frequently in the theories of English writers of the seventeenth century; essentially the solution adopted in England by the Toleration Act of 1689 is Erastian.

Erastians believe that the only way to secure religious peace is by giving the state control of religion; national churches are therefore Erastian in character. Most Erastians espoused this belief in the hope that the state could enforce either a comprehension of different beliefs within the state church or a toleration of them outside the state church. Such were the hopes of men like Bacon and Vane. The hope of toleration did not require that an Erastian be a skeptic; on the contrary, some of them, such as Vane and Goodwin, were men of deep faith. But in other cases Erastianism arose, not out of concern for toleration, but out of a real conviction that the state must be supreme. Thus there could be an extremely wide variance between the views of a Vane and those of a Hobbes. Vane, to be sure, wanted a state religion controlled by Parliament; but to him it was a true faith which was to be thus controlled, and he thought it could be done without the loss of religious truth or vitality. To Hobbes, who was not interested in religion in itself, a state church was a convenient device to lend additional support and strength to the state. The Hobbesian church is thus a church, as we have seen, equally devoid of vitality and truth.

The Erastian solution has a long history in England, for the Anglican church has always been an Erastian institution; necessarily so, for the position of the English monarchs as heads of the church and the later lack of constitutional restraints on a supreme parliament have meant that in actuality the political authorities are in a position to rule the church, even to regulate its dogmas. Divine right was an

Erastian doctrine; so is parliamentary supremacy. The fact that there has always been opposition within the church to this status does not change the situation. In 1857 the Divorce Act, later attempts to force free communion on the church as the right of every Englishman, and the refusal of Parliament to assent to changes in the Book of Common Prayer are all illustrations of this point.[14]

Other examples of Erastianism are the Lutheran state churches and the Eastern Church under the Czars, but these are outside the scope of this analysis.

Erastianism had some vogue in colonial America, particularly in Virginia where the House of Burgesses did not give up its right to legislate on religious questions until the Act for Religious Freedom was passed in 1785; technically it has not done so to this day. However, Erastianism seems unlikely in this country today. The divisions of Christianity and the jealousy of the churches for their own independence militate against any such state control of religion. Yet in the field of education, at least, the Erastian solution is not too far-fetched; religious education in public schools has always been the religious education that the state has been willing to allow, not what the churches have desired. It is probable that the same situation might eventually occur were the parochial schools to be financially supported by the government. Such a condition would be essentially Erastian.

8

Total conflict can obviously develop into totalitarianism; it is not so obvious, but it is nevertheless true, that total identification and Erastianism can do so also. This is because identification has already granted half the requirements of totalitarianism when it concedes that the state has of right an interest in the religious welfare of its people. Erastianism goes even farther by giving the state the right to control which religion shall be permitted, a doctrine which logically leads to the idea that the state can deny the right of *any* religion to exist, or at least to exist except on the state's own terms.

This is essentially what took place both in Germany and in Russia where the people were habituated to the idea that the state should control the religious organization. But totalitarian philosophy does not stop with the mere denial of religious rights. It has also its positive side. For the very word "totalitarian" implies an attempt to mold and control the total man, his soul and his character no less than his body and his economic activities. In the spirit of Hegel's dictum that the state is "the march of God on earth," the totalitarian philosophy envisages the state as a spiritual organism in which the citizen finds the entire meaning of life. The state does not deny religion—it *is* religion. The state is the object of reverence; the state is the highest moral authority. Morality in its largest sense consists in total submission to the state, and in detail it exists only as defined by the state.

It is the practically unanimous judgment of observers, therefore, that the Nazi state and the Communist dogma have the main essentials of a religious faith and that they consciously have attempted to substitute themselves for the traditional religions. In such a state, of course, there can be no freedom of religion at all, much less any possibility of separation.

We should perhaps not be too hasty in our conclusion that this cannot happen in the United States. While it may be doubtful that revealed religion as we know it is necessary for the maintenance of moral standards in a political community,[15] it seems almost beyond doubt that if freedom is to exist in the community, some agency besides the state must be in a position to exert moral influence. The modern tendency to justify the church's existence primarily on the grounds of its necessity for morality is a dangerous one, for the position is open to grave attack. But once we realize the fact that in the absence of the church one of the strongest bulwarks against the assumption by the state of *all* morality is gone, we can proceed to justify the persistence of strong religious organizations as a necessity for freedom and a democratic political order. Democracy depends on the existence of groups within it which are in a position to criticize the state not only on political but also on moral grounds. Strong religious groups are one symptom of a healthy democratic political life. We can well use the opposition between church and state in morality in the same way we use the opposition of the minority political party to the administration in power politically.

It is commonplace to point out that all modern states have increased in power as a result of increasing industrialization and of the wars of the twentieth century. It is likewise often pointed out that the increasing democracy which is a part of American history, combined with the growth of mass-communications media, "scientific" propaganda, and the comparative failure of our school systems properly to prepare our mass citizenry for its role in democratic government, all lead in the direction of an increasing reliance on the state. This increasing reliance can easily be transformed into a belief in loyalty to the state as the only and all-consuming loyalty of human beings. Indeed the recent loyalty campaigns seemed to proceed on this assumption. The same trends of thought in other countries have produced a phenomenon sometimes called "totalitarian democracy"—totalitarianism based on mass enthusiasm and support with suppression of "competing" social institutions.

To give the state any formal control over religion—for instance, as in religious education—would be a further step toward such all-embracing governmental power. Of course no one proposes giving the state *control* over religious education; but it seems almost inevitable, given the trend referred to above, that bringing religion in any guise into the public schools might eventually mean governmental control of the content, time, and teaching of religious education. The same can be said of governmental financial aid to parochial schools.

Separation of church and state, then, regardless of its other virtues, may be regarded as a major bulwark of the liberal democratic state as opposed to totalitarian democracy.[16]

9

As I have remarked previously, complete separation of church and state in the sense of the utter absence of any interaction or conflict seems to be impossible, particularly in the Western World. Christianity as well as the state claims the right to control the acts of men. Partial separation is an important principle not because it ends, but because it minimizes, conflict.

However, to concede merely that conflict will still exist even when state and church are independent leaves us without a real solution. The conflicts between church and state through history have seldom been based on the assumption that each did not have a separate sphere of legitimate action, but have instead turned on the questions of where the boundaries shall be and of who shall decide disputes arising which concern both; i.e., who shall *draw* the boundaries. Merely to assert a doctrine of separation does not answer these questions.

Those who believe in separation, then, must go a step farther. The two possible judges in case of conflict are necessarily the parties to the dispute, for there are no higher agencies to which to turn. Modern Roman Catholic political theory seems to assert the right of the church as the divine agent of God on earth to make the decision. Secular political philosophy, especially in America in the hands of Jefferson and the "Roosevelt Court," maintains the opposite: the state is of right the judge. Those of us who agree with the Jeffersonian tradition have no reasoned philosophical basis for our position, for the writer of the Act for Religious Freedom and our modern court justices seem to have arrived at the concept almost intuitively. The Roman Catholic church, on the other hand, has built up a reasoned political theory in which its views are contained.[17] It is the object of this study, in the light of historical research and philosophy, to begin the construction of a sound theoretical basis for the doctrine that modern democratic states should and must exercise. the right of decision when the church and the state come into conflict. In the modern religiously heterogeneous state this seems to be the only democratically expedient solution, but as a political principle it must have a sounder foundation; it must be seen to be not only politically expedient but also philosophically desirable.

136

7

A Modern American Theory
of Separation

A NY ATTEMPT to construct a theory of church-state relations, from the standpoint of the political philosopher, must guard against two major assumptions: that his theory can be arrived at apart from a general theory of what the state is and what the church is; and that any church or any religion holds all religious truth. Perhaps it is a mistake to *assume* even that religious truth exists. On the other hand, he must equally try not to assume either that *no* church holds any religious truth or that *no* religious truth exists. The political philosopher, *as* political philosopher, is qualified to construct a theory of the state, but he is not a theologian and is in no position to judge of either the existence or the value of religious truth.[1]* This statement is made in the full knowledge that such complete ethical neutrality is impossible. All men, theologians or not, who have studied philosophy and politics are bound to have personal views as to the relations of man and the world to the supernatural. No man can be completely objective; we are all participants, as Shakespeare pointed out, in life's drama. There is no audience, no critic, except one who shares the faults of the players

* Notes to this chapter begin on page 168.

because he is also one of them. Therefore I do not claim to have achieved the objectivity which is necessary and which must be sought after; I only claim to have made the attempt. Its success must be judged by others.

1

The concept of "state," while it seems to have been indispensable in modern political theory, must always be recognized as no more than a concept if the student is a believer in democracy. No one has ever seen a state; it cannot be described, as a government or a church or a labor union can. It should also be kept in mind that the traditional connection of the theories of state and sovereignty, which was begun by Jean Bodin, has no meaning in a democracy and has led many democratic thinkers astray. As a consequence, some recent writers have suggested that we cannot use the state concept at all in a democratic society, that it has no relevance.[2] Others retain the state but distinguish sharply between different kinds of states—a semantic device which has practically the same effect.[3] It is not necessary here to enter into this controversy; it is sufficient that we realize that throughout the ensuing discussion, unless specifically labelled otherwise, the term "state" means the *democratic* state and particularly the *constitutionally limited* democratic state.

There has been a widespread tendency in political theory to confuse the state with the government on the one hand and with the society (community) on the other. We must begin therefore by denying that the state is society or that government is the state.

If we accept MacIver's definition of the state as "men organized under government," and add his qualification that this is only one particular organization among many,[4] we shall avoid confusing the state with society. The state, in short, is merely one of the manifestations of social life. It cannot, under this definition, embrace all the community's activities. This is the fundamental difference between the totalitarian and democratic concepts of the state. Since the democratic state is only one phase of social activity, for one set of purposes among many, the loyalties of human beings cannot be wholly absorbed by it. The democratic state cannot be totalitarian.

The definition of the state as one social organization necessarily means that there must be others. The church is one of the most important of these. Here MacIver's fruitful concept of the "multi-group" society is relevant.[5] In short, this concept is that men always live in groups, and that most men belong to more than one group— state, business, club, church, city, social set, and so on. No one of these groups, moreover, can absorb all the rest or wholly control the social life of man. Men do not live exclusively for any one group.[6]

In addition, MacIver's theory assumes that no man is completely absorbed in society itself; each man always remains to some extent an individual with some autonomy in (at least) thought and motivation. His life in any group has personal aims and personal meaning as well as social; even in religion he seeks personal satisfaction (salvation). And the aims of the group, if attained, are enjoyed not by the group but by the individuals composing it.

Put into moral terms this theory assumes that neither the state nor even the more inclusive community itself is absolute, for they have life only in the individuals who form them. Morality as an absolute is not a community concept any more than it is a state concept. The community is a sort of cooperative attempt to reach ultimate morality—it does not embody it.

The idea of a multi-group society may seem to run counter to the prevailing theory that political stability requires unity (sometimes called "basic consensus"). Without denying that some unifying idea is needed for the maintenance of the political community, one may doubt that this requirement is as important as has sometimes been assumed. As Friedrich has pointed out, all Americans do not agree on the meaning of democracy itself, which is certainly a "fundamental."[7] In fact, it seems more likely that democratic society assumes a certain amount of *lack* of agreement; it is only totalitarian states which find it necessary to insist on agreement. This is particularly clear in religion. No one will deny that religion is fundamental, or at least that it has been fundamental in all civilization so far. Yet insistence on agreement in religion in Western history has led only to conflict and even to revolution. Only when men could "agree to disagree" in religion was the rise of democratic freedom in England possible. For our purposes this is all we need to establish.

It indicates that no democratic society can insist on religious unity, that such insistence breeds only conflict, and that in the modern world religious unity is not a prerequisite for political unity. Such religious unity as exists must be voluntary.

This is only to say that no state can entirely reconcile all the conflicts within it; in the democratic state the attempt to do so can lead only to the loss of democracy. In religion the allowance by the state of a free play of opinion is necessary for the maintenance of democracy. Not only would enforced unity destroy the democratic state, it would render the religion sterile; for religion, like most "voluntary" activities,[8] depends largely upon spontaneity for its vitality. Religious differences exist in any modern multi-group society, and they are largely irreconcilable.

The really vital religious groups in our history have been those which were opposed to government control, not those which were allied with government. The teeming nonconformist groups produced the English civil war; the early fervor of New England stemmed from its opposition to the established church; and the rapid growth of the sects forced toleration and was important in bringing separation to the United States. On the other hand, the established churches were always on the defensive and losing ground, and this was particularly true of the Congregational church in New England after 1700 and of the Anglican church in Virginia and other American colonies.

It was such opposition by dissenting religious groups to the autocratic governments of the seventeenth and eighteenth centuries which played a major role in bringing about the birth of the democratic state. Churches closely allied with government were never on the side of democracy; the long fight for life by persecuted faiths went hand in hand with the rise of more democratic governments. For religion, then, freedom is more important than uniformity under modern world conditions. As Rommen points out, the test of a good state is not the degree of homogeneity that exists within it, for that would be to make totalitarianism ideal. This is also the argument that Aristotle brings against Plato's *Republic*: Plato's proposals, first, cannot achieve the objective of unity; and second, unity in itself is not a valid end for a political association.[9] The objective

should be to allow as much freedom as possible and to have only
as much homogeneity as necessary. Men have many loyalties, and
these loyalties do not necessarily cause conflict; the good government
bends its efforts to avoiding such conflicts rather than to the elimination of all competing loyalties.[10]

Thus we posit a limited democratic state, limited as any democratic
state must be by the three facts that (1) it must recognize and
permit the existence of other groups in society which may be as
fundamental to that society as it is, (2) it cannot under any circumstances fulfill all the needs of its individual citizens, and (3) it
depends on the free play of opinion for its own maintenance.

2

The belief has been earlier indicated that the political theorist is
not in a very good position to judge the quality of religious knowledge, since he is not versed in theology. If he is also relatively
unversed in sociology—the position in which, regrettably, many
political theorists find themselves—he is similarly handicapped in
making an independent judgment of what the church really is and
what functions it fulfills in society. Yet any attempt to establish a
well-grounded theory of separation depends to a large extent on the
position which religion and the churches occupy. In this attempt
the author has tried to restrict himself to the factual position of the
Christian churches in Western history, particularly in the United
States. Recourse has been had mainly to churchmen's own ideas of
the church; sociological study has of necessity been minimized.

The fact that religion is not purely a subjective experience of the
individual has already been indicated.[11] From the further conclusion
that no individual completely loses his identity in any of his group
associations, it also follows that religion is not purely social.[12]
Religion is both an individual experience and a social relationship,
and these are characteristics which the statesman and the political
thinker must take into account. The fact that it does have an individual
aspect suggests that the designation of our problem as "church and
state" is incomplete and misleading, for it makes no reference to
the position of the individual. Our conflict is not merely between

two institutions, but between two sides of the individual—the political and the religious.

The church may be regarded as the institutional and social aspect of religion. As such it has social rights, just as has any other basic social association. The problem is complicated, however, by the fact that the individual also has rights which may sometimes conflict with those of the group. This problem becomes especially difficult in our secular society because of the large number of citizens who are attached to no religious group. If all citizens were members of one church, or even of *some* church, we could perhaps assume that their rights in religion were to some extent given up to the church, or at least expressed through the church organization. In other words, under such conditions the institutional right would tend to absorb and represent the individual right. But when many persons individually retain all their religious beliefs and rights, there tends to be at least an equality of right between the religious group and the unaffiliated individual, with the possibility of frequent conflict.

It has been said with some justice that separation in the United States has endowed the churches with freedom to the detriment of *individual* religious liberty.[13] It seems likely, however, that this result is due not to law or governmental act, but to a generally intolerant attitude in this country toward free-thinking—an intolerance perhaps stemming from the American reaction to the excesses of the French Revolution and from the longstanding connection in the public mind between religious and political radicalism. It does not seem as likely that this predominance of the organized form of religion is generic with separation; but American politics undeniably give great power to any organized group which is in a position to exert effective political pressure.

To the theologian or philosopher the church stands for a moral position which it claims is higher than that of the state. A believer in either natural law or God would perforce concede that such a higher morality exists, and even though he might not conclude that the church is the representative of the higher morality, he would be unlikely to affirm that the state is. This leads us to an important conclusion regarding the position of state and church. The state—at least the democratic state—does not represent or enforce absolute morality (a statement even the complete moral relativist would accept). Whether or not the church does is not determinative of the conclusion that in such a state there must be some standard other than that of the state itself. If there were no other morality (absolute or relative, as you will), the state would be in the absurd position of willy-nilly formulating and enforcing a morality which all agree is not absolute and which could not be judged by reference to any other standard. This would be the essence of totalitarianism, not democracy.

In this view the church as the representative of a morality other than that of the state occupies a crucial position in society. If it represents absolute morality, and infallibly, it provides a definite standard by which to judge the morality of the state and the actions of the state; if it represents merely *another* standard of morality, it still provides a necessary alternative to the state's course of action. Democracy depends greatly on the existence of such an alternative and on the maintenance of the freedom of the citizenry to choose this alternative in preference to that of the state.

It is true that modern multi-group society contains many different groups which also can provide alternative policy choices. Political parties are the most obvious and important examples. Yet this fact does not eliminate the importance of the church, for a multiplicity of alternatives is needed, if for no other reason than to avoid the polarity of two alternatives and the consequent labeling of one as white or pure, the other as black or sinful. Then, too, the political parties often represent mere choices between political expedients rather than real moral alternatives; and the political actions fostered by parties are those of compromise rather than moral choice. In a democracy such compromise is a necessity,[14] but moral choice is also necessary for human beings. The political party, then, provides a vehicle for *political* choice opposing the government in power; the church provides a means of *moral* choice. The existence of such a moral alternative to the state has historically given liberty its chance to grow, through the maintenance of an organization in society which can oppose the state on ethical grounds.[15]

For the church to maintain its position as the moral critic of the state independence is required. By being subject to, or closely identified with, the state, the church loses its own freedom to criticize in the same way in which a British cabinet member by remaining in the cabinet relinquishes his right publicly to oppose cabinet policies. The church thus needs separation if it is to fulfill its *moral* function in the modern democratic state. The only other possibility would be the supremacy of the church over the state in the moral realm; but this is impossible and undesirable unless (1) everyone belongs to the same church and (2) the church's voice is morally infallible. The first condition is patently lacking in modern America or elsewhere in the world; the second, in view of the many religious beliefs in the state and the frequent disagreements between them, cannot be assumed by any conscientious statesman in his public capacity. Church supremacy, subjection, or identity are all alike impossible under modern conditions.

The church is a free fellowship; it may formulate its own creed and determine and conduct its own organization; it may select and expel its own members. It may *not* exercise any control over anyone except its members, make its membership a requirement for any civil rights, or use legal compulsion of any kind. Nor may it require, in the name of religion, the state to observe its particular moral beliefs.

3

With this theory of the state and of the church in mind we may proceed to that of separation itself, with the hope that it may be firmly grounded in the political and religious realities of American life.

The state is a fundamental expression of human life in society, but as we have seen, other social groups are no less so. These other social groupings because of their fundamental quality have certain minimum rights which a democratic state can abrogate only at the price of ending its democratic existence. Chief among these is, of course, the right of existence; another is the right of free expression. The churches as they are members of this group of free societies partake of these rights. No democratic government can attempt to do away with them or with their exercise of their own forms of religious expression.

This, however, is only part of the story. As we have seen, human beings as individuals—that is, without consideration as members of free associations—have rights also, and these individual rights may be considered as in a sense more basic than the rights of groups. Certainly there is this added right of an individual: the right to join free associations, and it stems from his own right of free expression as well as from the right of the associations to exist.

These rights of individuals point to a fundamental reason why in a democratic state the state and the church must be as separate as possible. If the citizen has a right to join a voluntary group, he has the coordinate right to refrain from joining it and the right to leave it after he has joined it. If these rights be granted, it follows that no church, in theory (whatever may be the case in practice), can be coextensive with the state, for there are always either actual or potential non-members of the church. Therefore the state cannot in line with its function of espousing the common good recognize and advance any church officially, since in so doing it would not be working for the common good but rather for the good of a particular group which was actually or potentially smaller than the population of the state.

It is obvious then that the theory of separation assumes that only the state is composed of the same individuals that compose the social community. Only the state can therefore be regarded as a compulsory organization. Here arises the distinction between the state and the church. A child is born into a state—a fact which may not be changed; he is fated to live in a political society. The state to be a state must have legal jurisdiction over every person within its borders. The church, on the other hand, cannot in theory be composed of all the citizens, since any of them have the right to withdraw or refuse to join. The outstanding fact of the modern-day is that no one can escape political authority; he leaves one state's jurisdiction only to enter that of another. This is obviously not true of the church nor of any other grouping of men in society.[16]

Separation of church and state thus flows in theory from the distinction between a universal and a particular organization, which in turn gives rise to the distinction between compulsory and voluntary.[17]

The facts of American life have borne out this theory. At no time, obviously, have all Americans belonged to *the* church or to

145

any church. Thus it is not only theoretically a breach of democratic principle but empirically impossible, and even if possible, unwise, for the state to ally itself with a church.[18]

It will be said by some, however, that the church is of divine institution and thus holds a moral authority which distinguishes it from a "voluntary" organization.[19] This argument assumes, it seems, two things which cannot be accepted by the statesman in his public capacity. First, it assumes that the church's moral authority extends even to those who reject its very claim to that authority. For any church to exercise such authority over all citizens, therefore, would be to deny the individual the freedoms which have been previously established. Second, the argument assumes the church's own infallibility, for only if its moral judgments are infallible can its moral authority be binding.[20] If the church could err, for men to obey it when it did would for them to sin, in the view of God.[21] A democratic state cannot accept any religious pronouncement as infallible; to do so would be the very negation of democracy, particularly when, as often happens, the majority of the citizens do not accept either the theory of infallibility or the infallibility of any particular church or any particular judgment. The state is bound to regard all churches, all religious beliefs as being equal, not only with each other, but with a belief in *no* religion at all.

If the religious authority be not infallible, it has no right to claim that its moral judgments have any right to be enforced by the state, for the church is not then responsible to God, to its own members, or in any way to the nation's people. Only the assumption of infallibility can give its moral judgments any political value beyond their intrinsic merit from the political point of view.[22]

It may be objected at this point that religion is necessary for the common good and that the state's recognition of religion and promotion of it are actually for the public good, even though many in the public do not think so. This position, however, seems to me to beg the question; for even though it be conceded that religion is a necessity for the maintenance of social stability and morality, the question as to what *kind* of religion would still remain unanswered, and there would still be no reason for governmental action. After all, there are many kinds of activity which are good for society, but governments cannot be expected to promote or regulate all of them and still remain democratic. Democracy must always leave a large area of private voluntary activity even in things which are considered desirable or necessary from the public standpoint. If for no other reason, this must be done because, ordinarily, voluntary activities are more vital and enthusiastic than directed ones.

Additionally, it seems clear that for the government to aid "all religions" would involve political authority in wholly needless controversies over definition. What is a religion? Can the term include ethical culture societies? Masonic organizations? Cults such as "I AM"? Spiritualism? To raise such questions is to conclude almost automatically that the state should be left free from such affairs, both for our protection and for its own welfare.

Much of the opposition to official neutrality seems to stem from the common belief that neutrality is the same as opposition;[23] the Biblical judgment "He that is not with me is against me" is often quoted in this connection. Whether neutrality actually amounts to hostility, however, depends largely on circumstances; and the circumstances for such a situation do not exist in the United States. In practice neutrality gives the impression of *support of the status quo*. If most people are Christians, probably most schoolteachers are also, and if so, their influence, even without formal religious education, will inevitably be on the side of the churches. Nor does the objection that in university philosophy departments neutrality amounts to the freedom only to teach irreligion stand up under analysis. There is no reason at all why universities cannot hire philosophers who are Christians as well as those who are not. The fact that state universities do not give courses in Christianity does not, therefore, mean that Christianity must be unmentionable or even neutrally treated by individual teachers.

The state, therefore, limited as we have seen, is the only agency which expresses the political will of at least a majority of the citizenry. Since this is so, and since the decisions of a democratic state can be reversed by the use of the democratic processes which are open to churches and their members as they are to anyone else, it seems logical and necessary that in cases in which there is conflict between church and state, the organs of the state must assume the responsibility (however onerous it may be) and the right to decide the issue.[24]

No one, of course, questions the right of a church or any other voluntary group to demand of its members adherence to its standards of moral conduct and to its creed. The church can therefore forbid its members on pain of excommunication to drink or to teach evolution. It is the right of a church to enforce such ideas on the general populace which is in question. There would be no issue if the people as a whole accepted the particular standard, but in such a case there would be little need for the churches to make special efforts to secure legislation. For instance, monogamy is universally enforced in this country because it is generally accepted as being right, not because it is espoused by the Christian churches (although there is an obvious connection). Conversely, the failure of the prohibition amendment occurred because large numbers of people did not accept the standard which the churches sought to enforce.

Direct political action is barred to the churches by the separation theory. Organized religion is restricted to influence over society brought to bear through influence on its own membership and as a common "pressure group," not through organic connections with government or by right. The Catholic writer Sturzo recognizes this when he says that the power of the church today is not expressed in control of the state but in "spiritual power over the faithful as individuals."[25] The church works indirectly on the state through the Christian ideals of its members.

This conclusion results from the separation doctrine that in theory the church is never universal within any state. It is strongly reinforced by the fact that no church is *actually* universal, or even nearly so, in the modern United States. Whatever the ideal situation in the mind of the religious man, this fact must be accepted at least for the present.

On what ground can we expect the government of a country in which half the people are not even nominally Christians, to lay down policies which are specifically related to Christianity?[26]

This is an unpleasant fact for many Christians, but it must nevertheless be faced.

148

As members of the State we have to think and to vote for what is the wisest course in a nation of which many of the Christians refuse to submit to our discipline, and many are not Christian at all. As citizens we have no right or claim to appeal to motives specifically Christian, or to lay down lines of policy which have no meaning except from the standpoint of the . . . Church.[27]

Thus both theory and actuality deprive the church of the right to enforce her beliefs through legislation. As Figgis wisely concludes,

the business of Christians is with the moral standard of their own society church and with themselves as its members. The raising of that will gradually bring about the elevation of the great mass of those who do not belong to it.[28]

If the state remains, as it must if democracy is to be retained, within the limits outlined above, it can do no harm to the church and can be a positive protection both of church and individual rights. As the McCollum and Zorach cases illustrate, the state in exercising this responsibility must often draw a tenuous line between the rights of the individual and those of the religious association, but as pointed out above, the organization does not ordinarily lose by this process. If anything, organized groups gain at the expense of individual rights. In any case, if our argument has been sound, the state has no choice but to make the decision. As long as the remedial processes of democracy remain open, and the state protects the rights of minorities both individual and associated, the churches cannot complain of injustice. It is likely that any weakness of the church under such conditions will be the fault of the social environment and of the churches themselves, not that of the operation of the separation principle. Indeed, Winthrop Hudson has argued persuasively that church dependence on state support is a symptom of religious weakness.[29]

On the contrary, it is probable that the church can actually gain from separation. It can thus be free to perform its "personal" function of preparing individuals for salvation without interference from the state. It is thus left free to perform its "social" function as moral critic of state and society without being forced to degrade itself to the support of the lower morality of state or society.

It is also free to propagandize in its own cause and its own way, to teach its members as it wishes without governmental direction, to proselyte, to impose upon its members such discipline as it believes in and can enforce, and in general to conduct itself with a liberty that has been gained by no state church.

The individual gains in separation by the freedom from compulsion of his own religious conscience and of his religious actions. If to mere separation be added a genuine spirit of tolerance in the society, this legal freedom is enhanced by an actual social liberty which is the right of every social being.

Finally, the state gains undeniably from a policy of separation. It is thus relieved of the burden of attempting to do that of which it is generically incapable: judging of religious truth. It is relieved of the necessity of upholding a belief which many or most of its citizens may deny. It is relieved of a tremendous number of disputes which require either its decision or its acceptance of the church's decision. Such relief leads to a lessening of conflict in an absolute sense; the democratic structure also renders such conflicts as still may arise less explosive, for the intense antagonisms which religious controversy may generate cannot easily focus against the state and thus do not so readily lead to violent reactions against it. In a sense a democratic state may be regarded simply as the institutionalization of change. The only universally accepted requirement in the way of belief is a belief in the method of democracy.[30] It gains stability not by the uniform acceptance of certain "fundamentals," but rather by faith in a method which can adapt itself not only to differences in fundamental beliefs but also to changes in them. Separation is necessary to the democratic state, for it assures that the state can survive religious change; the state is tied to no religious orthodoxy, truth, or organization which may lose its hold on the people. The decline of the religious motive in American society is not due to separation but to this precise difference between the democratic state and the church: for the church has so far proved unable, in the opinion of many, to adapt itself to the great social changes of the last century.[31] It is well for the state that it has been largely unhindered by the churches in its own faltering efforts at adaptation.

It is to the self-interest of the state, as well as to that of the church, to uphold as strictly as possible the separation principle. For much of the life of democracy depends on the existence of legitimate opposition to the governmental courses of action. Only through such opposition and the publicity given to suggested alternatives is the public enabled to study intelligently the issues with which it is confronted. The moral—and perhaps often practical—alternatives advanced by the churches can only be provided by a church which is legally and morally free of the government. The church's freedom to oppose the government is inevitably lessened by every favor it accepts or begs.

There is a final reason why from the church's standpoint it cannot be closely allied with the state. We have already seen that the church does not contain all the citizens of the state, and therefore it does not have jurisdictional rights coextensive with those of the state. But there is an added factor which must be taken into account as long as national states exist. For religion—and especially the Christian religion (and the Catholic church particularly)—is not only intranational but supranational. The ecumenical movement of even the Protestant faiths transcends national boundaries. An international church cannot ally itself with any of the states in which it exists. To do so is to invite its own destruction. The divisions, north and south, of the great Protestant churches of America, which are only today being eliminated, were caused by just such identification with the political positions of the Union and the Confederacy. Perhaps the greatest strength of the Roman Catholic Church has been its determination to avoid any such identification, as indicated by its insistence on the maintenance of the Vatican City as an independent territorial base. Catholics could fight for Germany, Italy, or the Allied nations without destroying either their own religious membership or the fabric of the church itself. Protestants find this question particularly trying, especially when as citizens of a colonial power they go as missionaries to one of its restive colonies. For Protestant churches have had a tendency to identify themselves with the nations in which they exist—a tendency which has been damaging to them individually (particularly the Lutheran churches) and to Christianity in general.[32]

Conversely, it is apparently unwise for the state to ally itself

151

closely with a church that is international, thus raising the old (and in the modern world largely fallacious?) fear of control of the state by some foreign religious leader.

In cases of actual conflict between church and state, in which the state as of right makes a decision, it cannot be assumed, of course, that the actual decision will be "right," either politically or morally. There may even be extreme cases when disobedience is a moral duty of the church or the individual. But this does not and cannot derogate from the right of the state to make the decision. The choice of disobedience, even though inspired by duty, is not a right in the political sense; he who disobeys must be willing to take the consequences of his disobedience. If in the circumstances he can successfully, by revolt or appeal to popular sentiment, force a change in the decision, well and good. But if he is not successful in so doing, he must suffer the penalty. This may sound somewhat Hobbesian; yet it is in reality only to assert that the individual or group does not have the right to disobey as it pleases. Political order requires general obedience.[33] This problem as to when morality requires disobedience, when Christ must be placed before Caesar, is the most serious problem confronting the religious man. But as Locke so admirably stated, it does not arise nearly so often in a state where church and state are separated as it does where they are not.

It should be almost needless to add that this theory of separation assumes the existence of a fundamental social unity which unites all men regardless of religious belief.

Whether a man be an Anglican, a presbyterian, a congregationalist, a Catholic, a Jew, or even an atheist, he is a *socius*; and whatever his particular way of salvation, it must be accommodated to the requirements of the social order.[34]

Conclusion

THE PURPOSE OF THIS WORK has been to examine the principle of separation of church and state in its historical and philosophical contexts, while at the same time keeping a wary eye on modern American social realities, in order to find out whether the principle is still, today, one which is calculated to serve the best interests of the American citizen. Equally it has been my purpose to discover the actual content which can properly be associated with the symbolic phrase "separation of church and state."

The analysis indicates that the reasons for the existence of separation are as valid and important now as they were in 1790. Both philosophically and practically, alternative systems of church-state relationships have been seen to be impossible, or at least unnecessary and unwise, whether the question be viewed from the standpoint of the state, of the religious organization, or of the individual citizen.

The argument is basically a pluralist one: that the church as one of the great fundamental institutions of society should be treated with the respect due its importance rather than as a tool of state policy. Conversely, religion's independence of state control renders it incapable of subjecting the government to religious versions of wise policy. The state is unable to judge in religious matters; the church is just as incapable in political matters. What happens, however, when (as seems inevitable) the political and religious come into conflict? My answer has been that such conflicts must be settled by the state, since it is the only social agency which properly has jurisdiction of all citizens and institutions within the society. Such decisions, if the system is wisely constructed, will be made in a nonpolitical manner by a nonpolitical agency (insofar as these things are possible). In the United States such conflicts necessarily involve constitutional questions and are thus settled by decisions of the United States Supreme Court, a system which satisfies in most respects the need for a prompt, responsible, nonpolitical settlement.

These conclusions will not make everyone happy. There are those who claim for the state a total sovereignty which would be incompatible with a separation principle, even though I have granted that final decisions in cases of conflict must be made by the state. Such partisans of state power will, I am afraid, not be converted by my pluralistic approach any more than they have been convinced by the great pluralists of the past and present such as J. N. Figgis, Lord Lindsay, Sir Ernest Barker, or Professor R. M. MacIver.

On the other hand there are those (and they are many in the United States) who are sincerely convinced that a godless society is a doomed society, and who (wrongly, I believe) conclude from this premise that the state power should be used to reinforce religious belief in order to preserve the essentials of a religious society. Some of these people, though not all, are actually motivated not so much by a concern for the welfare of society as a whole as by an understandable fear for the future of their particular religious organization. Such partisans of particular brands of religion will not be satisfied with any solution short of active governmental aid in the propagation of religious beliefs.

Yet there remain between these extremes many people who are concerned for the welfare of the individual citizen and the rights we have come to associate with American citizenship; for the preservation of a political system safe from the emotional turmoils to which states in the past have been subjected because of their involvement in religious strife; and for the maintenance of the free church system which made America the most strongly Christian nation in the world during the nineteenth century. There is nothing irreligious about any of these concerns; indeed, all of them have been expressed many times by men whose attachment to Christianity was beyond question. It is to these people that the analysis contained in this book may prove most valuable, for if the argument is sound it provides them with the first completely reasoned theory of what I have herein called "partial separation" which has been produced in America since the time of Madison and Jefferson.

Nevertheless I am far from believing that all the answers are contained herein; this book is no universal solvent for the questions with which it deals. My purpose has been more to stimulate discussion than to end it. If that much is achieved the effort will have been worth while.

Notes

CHAPTER 1

1. John W. Allen, *English Political Thought, 1603-1660* (London, 1938), I, 7.

2. F. C. Montague, *The History of England from the Accession of James I to the Restoration (1603-1660)*, Vol. VII of *The Political History of England*, ed. William Hunt and Reginald Poole (12 vols.; London, 1920), p. 127.

3. There is some dispute among historians as to how much of a "villain" Laud actually was. The view here presented is fully elucidated in Wilbur K. Jordan, *The Development of Religious Toleration in England* (London, 1932), II, 115-117; in Thomas Lyon, *The Theory of Religious Liberty in England, 1603-39* (Cambridge, 1937), pp. 68-69; and in a good many other works. The opposing view according to which Puritan intolerance was more important than that of Laud is strongly presented in Allen, pp. 181 ff.

4. Henry M. Gwatkin, *Church and State in England to the Death of Queen Anne* (London, 1917), p. 266.

5. George M. Trevelyan, *England under the Stuarts* (14th ed.; New York, 1928), pp. 173-174. For a strongly opposing view see Brooks Adams, *The Emancipation of Massachusetts* (Boston, 1893), p. 7.

6. Probably the fullest treatment of latitudinarian thought is found in Jordan, II, 315 ff. See also Lyon, pp. 144-204; and Allen, pp. 229-252.

7. Erastianism is dealt with rather fully in the works cited in note 6.

8. These limitations are brought out particularly well in Jacob D. Hyman, *William Chillingworth and the Theory of Toleration* (Cambridge, Mass., 1931), pp. 57-63; see also works cited in note 6.

9. Puritan thought is dealt with more thoroughly in Chap. 2 below and see references there cited. Also see Jordan, II, *passim*.

10. Independent thought is fully treated in Jordan, II, 220-257.

11. Separatist thinking is dealt with in Jordan, II, 216-258, and in Lyon, pp. 77-108.

12. For fuller treatment see Jordan, II, 258-310, and Lyon, pp. 109-142.

13. Roger Williams, *The Bloudy Tenent of Persecution for cause of Consciense Discussed,* ed. Edward B. Underhill (London, 1848), pp. 215, 266. See also James E. Ernst, *The Political Thought of Roger Williams* (Seattle, 1929), pp. 29, 62, 141, 176.

14. Williams, p. 9; also see pp. 128, 221.

15. *Ibid.,* pp. 46-47; see also pp. 99, 331-332.

16. *Ibid.,* p. 63.   17. *Ibid.,* pp. 87, 317-318.

18. David Masson, *The Life of John Milton* (new ed.; London, 1896), III, 118. This apparently depends upon the interpretation given to Williams, p. 264. See Ernst, p. 161.

19. Williams, p. 1.   20. *Ibid.,* pp. 169, 262-263.

21. *Ibid.,* pp. 147 ff., 157, 170, 340-342, and especially 304.

22. *Ibid.,* p. 1; see also pp. 100, 131, 294.

23. See Masson, III, p. 118; and Ernst, p. 162.

24. Williams, p. 285; see also pp. 142, 287, 353-356.

25. This does not imply that the writer agrees with all of Williams's conclusions. Some of them will be critically discussed in a later section of this book.

26. Williams, pp. 2, 156.

27. *Ibid.,* pp. 2, 17, 140, 245. And see Williams, *The Bloody Tenent yet More Bloody; by Mr. Cottons endevour to wash it white in the Blood of the Lambe; . . .* (London, 1652), Introduction.

28. Williams, *Bloudy Tenent of Persecution,* p. 320.   29. *Ibid.,* pp. 2, 64.

30. Don M. Wolfe, *Milton in the Puritan Revolution* (New York, 1941), pp. 70-71.

31. Attention should be called to a recent and sophisticated analysis of Williams's thought which differs in some respects from the interpretation here given. See Perry Miller, *Roger Williams* (Indianapolis, 1953).

32. On this point, see Arthur Barker, *Milton and the Puritan Dilemma, 1641-1660* (Toronto, 1942), pp. 93 ff., 128, 235, 242; Jordan, III, 203 f.; Wolfe, pp. 113, 118.

33. John Milton, "Areopagitica," *The Prose Works of John Milton,* ed. J. A. St. John (London, 1909), II, 74.

34. *Ibid.,* p. 89.   35. *Ibid.,* p. 86.   36. *Ibid.,* p. 97.

37. And even on freedom of the press Milton advocated only freedom from previous restraint. See *ibid.,* p. 55.

38. *Ibid.,* p. 97.   39. Barker, p. 118; see also pp. 235, 245.

40. Milton, "A Treatise of Civil Power in Ecclesiastical Causes; . . . ," *op. cit.,* p. 547.

41. Milton. "Of True Religion, Heresy, Schism, Toleration; . . . ," *op. cit.,* p. 510.

42. Milton, "Treatise of Civil Power," p. 529.

43. Milton, "Of True Religion," p. 511.   44. *Ibid.,* p. 514.

45. Milton, "Areopagitica," p. 92.

46. Barker, pp. 95-97.   47. *Ibid.,* p. 235.

48. *Ibid.,* p. 245. For further reading on Milton's beliefs see Jordan, IV, 203-230; Masson; Wolfe, pp. 94-118; and Allen, pp. 326-336.

49. Gilbert Burnet, *The History of My Own Times,* ed. Thomas Burnet (London, 1753), I, 262.

50. George P. Gooch, "Hobbes," *Proceedings of the British Academy, London,* XXV (1939), 85, says: "Loving intellectual liberty as much as any of his contemporaries, he felt nevertheless that self-government was a prize beyond our grasp. Order was heaven's first law, and no price was too high to obtain it. Anarchy was a ferocious animal which could only be kept at bay by the lash of an autocrat."

51. Thomas Hobbes, "Philosophical Rudiments Concerning Government and

Society," *The English Works of Thomas Hobbes of Malmesbury,* ed. William Molesworth (London, 1841), II, 221.

52. Hobbes, *The Elements of Law, Natural and Politic,* ed. Ferdinand Tonnies (Cambridge, 1928), p. 114.

53. *Ibid.,* p. 124.

54. *Ibid.;* and see "Philosophical Rudiments," p. 168.

55. Hobbes, "Leviathan; or, the Matter, Form, and Power of a Commonwealth, Ecclesiastical and Civil," *The English Works of Thomas Hobbes,* III, 165.

56. Hobbes, "Philosophical Rudiments," p. 219; cf. p. 295.

57. *Ibid.,* p. 271.   58. Hobbes, *Elements of Law,* p. 132.

59. Hobbes, "Leviathan," p. 460; and see p. 355.

60. Hobbes, "Philosophical Rudiments," p. 278.

61. Hobbes, "Leviathan," p. 492.   62. Hobbes, *Elements of Law,* p. 143.

63. Burnet, I, 262.   64. Hobbes, "Leviathan," pp. 98-99.

65. *Ibid.,* p. 103.   66. Jordan, IV, 307.

67. A. S. Seaton, *The Theory of Toleration under the Later Stuarts* (Cambridge, 1911), p. 81.

68. *Ibid.,* p. 83. Herbert W. Schneider, *The Puritan Mind* (New York, 1930), p. 13, remarks, "few objected to his absolutism but all to his secularism."

69. George P. Gooch, *Political Thought in England from Bacon to Halifax* (London, 1914), p. 121. And see Hugh F. Russell Smith, *Harrington and His Oceana* (Cambridge, 1914), p. 163.

70. James Harrington, "Valerius and Publicola, Or, the True Form of a Popular Commonwealth," *The Oceana of James Harrington, and His Other Works . . . ,* ed. John Toland (London, 1700), p. 489. See also Harrington's "A System of Politics Delineated in short and easy Aphorisms," *ibid.,* p. 516.

71. Harrington, "A System of Politics," pp. 506-507.

72. Russell Smith, p. 58. He excluded "Jews because they never mixed with nations that gave them protection, Papists because they owed allegiance to a foreign potentate, idolators because, like Robespierre, he believed in the supreme necessity of religion for securing social order."

73. Harrington, "The Commonwealth of Oceana," p. 89.   74. *Ibid.,* p. 127.

75. Harrington, "A System of Politics," pp. 505-506.

76. Harrington, "The Commonwealth of Oceana," p. 58.

77. *Ibid.,* p. 88; see also p. 127.   78. *Ibid.,* p. 127.

79. For further discussion of Harrington's thought refer to Russell Smith, *Harrington,* and Jordan, IV, 283-290.

80. Henry Vane, "A Healing Question propounded and resolved . . . ," *Old South Leaflets* (Boston, n.d.), Vol. I, No. 6, pp. 5, 7.

81. See Jordan, IV, 9-17.   82. Burnet, I, 128.

83. For details see Gwatkin, pp. 353 f.

84. Seaton, p. 224: "It was no longer a question of whether the Dissenters should receive toleration or not, rather the Church and the King were in excited competition as to which should have the honour of bestowing it upon them."

85. William Penn, "The Great Case of Liberty of Conscience. Once more briefly Debated and Defended . . . (1670)," *A Collection of the Works of William Penn* (London, 1726), I, *passim.*

86. Penn, "England's Present Interest Considered, with Honour to the Prince, and Safety to the People (1675)," *ibid., passim.*

87. Penn, "Good Advice to the Church of England, Roman-Catholick, and Protestant Dissenter . . . (1687)," *ibid.,* II, 750.

88. *Ibid.,* p. 772. Williams had maintained this much earlier; see his *Bloudy Tenent of Persecution,* p. 287.

89. Penn, *The Frame of Government of the Province of Pennsilvania* (1682), p. 11.

90. Russell Smith, *The Theory of Religious Liberty in the Reigns of Charles II and James II* (Cambridge, 1911), pp. 22, 52.

91. *Ibid.*, p. 2.

92. Harold J. Laski, *Political Thought in England from Locke to Bentham* (New York, 1920), p. 57.

93. "The Fundamental Constitutions of Carolina," *Old South Leaflets* (Boston, n.d.), Vol. VII, No. 172, pp. 95-109.

94. John Locke, *Letter Concerning Toleration*, ed. Charles L. Sherman (New York, 1937), pp. 210-213.

95. *Ibid.*, p. 208.   96. *Ibid.*, p. 210.   97. *Ibid.*, pp. 219-220.

98. A thorough treatment of Locke's thought on toleration may be found in Seaton, pp. 237-273.

99. For details see W. E. H. Lecky, *A History of England in the Eighteenth Century* (New York, 1879), I, 104; or Trevelyan, *England under the Stuarts*, pp. 469-475.

CHAPTER 2

1. See particularly his *Orthodoxy in Massachusetts, 1630-1650; A Genetic Study* (Cambridge, Mass., 1933).

2. Miller, p. 84.

3. William Ames, *Conscience with the Power and Cases Thereof* . . . , quoted in Miller, p. 86.

4. Ames, quoted Miller, p. 92. Even in New England this loyalty was never renounced. Miller (p. 158) says that Roger Williams's banishment really occurred because he insisted that they had actually separated. "Cotton could proudly point to [the banishment] . . . as a sign that New England had not renounced the Church of England."

5. Ames, quoted Miller, p. 95.

6. Brooks Adams, *The Emancipation of Massachusetts* (Boston, 1893), p. 7. This argument is a valuable addition to that advanced by the English historians cited in Chap. 1.

7. James T. Adams, *The History of New England*, Vol. I: *The Founding of New England* (Boston, 1921), pp. 122-143, strongly advances this opinion.

8. Miller, p. 51.

9. Miller, p. 100. This volume treats Puritan motivation very well, pp. 96-100. Cf. J. T. Adams, pp. 142-144; Thomas J. Wertenbaker, *The First Americans, 1607-1690*, Vol. II of *A History of American Life*, ed. A. M. Schlesinger and D. R. Fox (13 vols., New York, 1927-1948), pp. 88-90; Wertenbaker, *The Founding of American Civilization; The Puritan Oligarchy* (New York, 1947), pp. 29-31.

10. Ezra H. Byington, *The Puritan in England and New England* (Boston, 1896), p. 181.

11. J. T. Adams, p. 80; cf. Byington, p. 2.

12. Edward Eggleston, *The Beginners of a Nation* (New York, 1897), p. 109.

13. George E. Ellis, *The Puritan Age and Rule in the Colony of Massachusetts Bay* (Boston, 1888), p. 168. Cf. Wertenbaker, *Puritan Oligarchy*, p. 26. They could not, of course, completely eliminate their English background in law and politics, so that this theory was never put fully into practice; see Charles E. Merriam, *A History of American Political Theories* (New York, 1902), pp. 3-5.

14. See, for instance, the story of the mouse and the snake in John Winthrop, *Journal, History of New England*, ed. J. K. Hosmer (2 vols., New York, 1908), I, 83 f.

15. To every man they gave the right, as Schlamann ironically puts it, "to open his Bible and read out of it, those things which they themselves had read." Ernest A. Schlamann, "The Puritan Fathers and Religious Liberty" (unpublished thesis, University of Chicago, 1895), p. 2.

16. J. T. Adams, p. 79. Merriam (p. 5) says that "there was never, perhaps, a body of clergy that exercised greater influence on affairs of state. . . ." Cf. Ellis, pp. 34 f., 172 ff.

17. J. T. Adams, p. 162; cf. Ellis, pp. 169, 183.

18. J. T. Adams, p. 143.

19. Mecklin, in his penetrating sociological study, states: "The intolerance of Massachusetts was not that of individuals primarily but was ingrained in her institutions and prevailing way of life. It is a familiar fact that there is no form of intolerance so truculent and at the same time so insidiously dangerous as that of an institution. The institution must assume its enduring worth and its authoritative finality. By its very nature it stands opposed to the fluctuating opinions of minorities. . . . The intolerance of the Bay province was an integral part of the very spirit and philosophy of its institutional forms. . . ." John M. Mecklin, *The Story of American Dissent* (New York, 1934), p. 187.

20. Endicott found it necessary to deport the Brownes, two Anglicans who came to Massachusetts with the first settlers; see Winthrop, I, 52 ed. n. In 1637 new additions to the Hutchinson party were forbidden to stay by Winthrop; see Winthrop, I, 226.

21. B. Adams, p. 116.

22. Nathaniel Ward, *Simple Cobler of Agawam,* quoted in Perry Miller and Thomas H. Johnson, *The Puritans* (New York, 1938), pp. 226, 230, 232.

23. This refers to his conduct in the Antinomian dispute in which he was a friend of Mrs. Hutchinson, who regarded herself as his disciple. But when he found himself in a distinct minority, opposed by both ministers and government, he talked his way out and ended by himself making the speech which expelled the unfortunate woman from the Boston church.

24. Henry B. Parkes, "John Cotton and Roger Williams Debate Toleration, 1644-1652," *New England Quarterly,* IV (1931), 748.

25. John Cotton, *Bloudy Tenent Washed,* quoted *ibid.,* p. 747.

26. Cotton, letter to Sir Richard Saltonstall, quoted in J. T. Adams, p. 261.

27. *Ibid.* He also maintained that persecution was not of a sinner's conscience, but of his sin against his conscience; a heretic, according to this theory, was a willful sinner. Cf. Merriam, pp. 10-14.

28. Wertenbaker, *Puritan Oligarchy,* p. vii.

29. Sanford H. Cobb, *The Rise of Religious Liberty in America* (New York, 1902), p. 111.

30. Joseph H. Crooker, *The Winning of Religious Liberty* (Boston, 1918), pp. 252-253.

31. Portions of the act establishing toleration are as follows:

"That whatsoever pson or psons within this Province . . . shall from henceforth blaspheme God, that is Curse him, or deny our Savior Jesus Christ to bee the sonne of God, or shall deny the holy Trinity the ffather sonne and holy Ghost, or the Godhead of any of the said Three psons of the Trinity or the Unity of the Godhead, or shall use or utter any reproachfull Speeches, words or languages concerning the said Holy Trinity, or any of the said three psons thereof, shalbe punished with death and confiscation or forfeiture of all his or her lands and goods . . .

". . . That whatsoever pson or psons shall . . . use or utter reproachfull words or Speeches concerning the blessed Virgin Mary the Mother of our Saviour or the holy Apostles or Evangelists or any of them" shall be fined, publicly whipped, imprisoned or banished, according to the number of offences.

The act also forbids calling anyone a "heretick, Schismatick, Idolator, puritan, Independent, Prespiterian, popish priest, Jesuite, Jesuited papist," etc., forbids anyone to "pphane the Sabbath . . . by frequent swearing, drunkennes or by any uncivill or disorderly recreacon, or by working . . . when absolute necessity does not require it," and provides that no one shall be "troubled, Molested or discountenanced for or in respect of his or her religion nor in the free exercise thereof . . . nor any way compelled to the belief or exercise of any other Religion against his or her consent. . . . " (*Archives of Maryland*, Assembly, I, 244-247.)

The last sentence quoted is at strange variance with the rest of the act and therefore illustrates sharply the limitations of most seventeenth-century thought.

32. Vernon L. Parrington, *Main Currents in American Thought*, Vol. I: *The Colonial Mind* (New York, 1927), p. 62.

33. Mecklin, p. 49.

34. Quoted in Cobb, p. 431; the date 1647 is assigned by Samuel H. Brockunier, *The Irrepressible Democrat, Roger Williams* (New York, 1940), p. 178.

35. *Records of the Colony of Rhode Island and Providence Plantations*, I, 376; also see pp. 374, 378.

36. *Records of Rhode Island*, II, 1. See also the petition to King Charles I, I, 490.

37. It is cited as good law in Crooker, p. 192. The newer view is taken by Cobb, pp. 437 f.; the Catholic writer Joseph F. Thorning, *Religious Liberty in Transition* (New York, 1931), pp. 139 f.; and the state's own view in *Records of Rhode Island*, II, 36 f.

38. William G. Torpey, *Judicial Doctrines of Religious Rights in America* (Chapel Hill, 1948), p. 14.

39. Dutch West India Company to Stuyvesant, April 16, 1663, quoted in William W. Sweet, *Religion in Colonial America* (New York, 1942), p. 152.

40. Evarts B. Greene, *Religion and the State* (New York, 1941), p. 61.

41. Sweet, pp. 334 ff.

CHAPTER 3

1. Thomas Jefferson, *Writings*, ed. H. A. Washington (9 vols., New York, 1853-54), I, 39.

2. *Virginia Statutes at Large* (Hening), I, 49.

3. Washington later withdrew his support.

4. *Va. Stats. at Lge.*, XII, 84-86.

5. Reprinted in Charles F. James, *Documentary History of the Struggle for Religious Liberty in Virginia* (Lynchburg, Va., 1900), pp. 222-225.

6. *The Writings of James Madison*, ed. Gaillard Hunt (9 vols., New York, 1900-1910), I, 143 f.; cf. pp. 108 f., 122 ff.

7. *Ibid.*, I, 153 ff.   8. *Ibid.*, I, 173 ff.

9. *A Memorial of the Convention of the Presbyterian Church*, August 13, 1785, reprinted in James, pp. 227 ff.

10. Cited in H. J. Eckenrode, *Separation of Church and State in Virginia* (Richmond, 1909), p. 110.

11. Cited *ibid.*, p. 107.

12. Cited in W. W. Sweet, *Religion in Colonial America* (New York, 1942), p. 339.

13. Madison, *Memorial and Remonstrance*, cited in James, p. 258.

14. *Va. Stats. at Lge.*, XII, 85; Locke, *Letter Concerning Toleration*, ed. C. L. Sherman (New York, 1937), pp. 210-213.

15. Jefferson, *Writings*, VIII, 400; Montesquieu, *The Spirit of Laws*, ed. J. V. Prichard (London, 1878), II, 138.

16. Jefferson, *Writings*, V, 471.   17. *Ibid.*, VIII, 400.

18. *Memorial and Remonstrance*, p. 257.   19. *Ibid.*

20. *Va. Stats. at Lge.*, XII, 86.   21. *Memorial and Remonstrance*, pp. 257-258.

22. Sadie Bell, *The Church, the State, and Education in Virginia* (Philadelphia, 1930), pp. 176-180.

23. Jefferson, *Writings*, VI, 267; cf. Bell, pp. 199-203, 374-376.

24. See quotation *infra* p. 71. Madison's view was similar on this point. See his letter to Edward Livingston, *Writings*, III, 273, in which he also opposed the payment of chaplains for Congress by the government; and see his *Detached Memoranda*, quoted in J. M. O'Neill, *Religion and Education under the Constitution* (New York, 1949), pp. 106-107. Of the philosophical development of Madison surprisingly little seems to be known. It seems probable, however, that his ideas on the problem of church and state were (as in the case of Jefferson) derived as a part of his general political theory developed through wide reading and in harmony with the intellectual climate of the times. It is also true that Madison was dependent for his political support on the favor of an electoral district which was strongly dissenting and thus against the Establishment. His studies under his Scotch schoolmaster Donald Robertson were apparently a strong influence in his intellectual development. Brant believes, also, that Madison's idea of the value to liberty of a multiplicity of religious sects was gleaned from a surreptitious reading of the forbidden Voltaire while the budding statesman was a student at New Jersey College (now Princeton University). See Irving Brant, *James Madison, the Virginia Revolutionist* (Indianapolis, 1941), pp. 58-61, 68-71, 111-122, 127-131; and Edward M. Burns, *James Madison, Philosopher of the Constitution* (New Brunswick, N. J., 1938), pp. ix, 1, 25-26, 83.

25. Jefferson, *The Commonplace Book*, ed. Gilbert Chinard (Baltimore, 1926), p. 291; cf. Montesquieu, Vol. II, Bk. XXVI, Chap. 2.

26. Jefferson, *Commonplace Book*, pp. 251, 362-363.

27. *Va. Stats. at Lge.*, XII, 85.   28. *Memorial and Remonstrance*, p. 257.

29. *Writings of Madison*, I, 214.   30. Jefferson, *Writings*, I, 45.

31. Allan Nevins, *The American States during and after the Revolution, 1775-1788* (New York, 1924), 436.

32. Eckenrode, pp. 58-61.

33. However, Connecticut still refused full equality to non-Christians and New Hampshire to non-Protestants.

34. Jonathan Elliott (ed.), *The Debates in the Several State Conventions on the Adoption of the Federal Constitution . . . Together with the Journal of the Federal Convention* (5 vols., Washington, 1836-45), III, 204.

35. *The Works of Thomas Jefferson*, ed. Paul Leicester Ford (12 vols., New York, 1904-1905), V, 25.

36. *Writings of Madison*, I, 424.

37. *Ibid.* The Massachusetts objection here referred to by Madison was also voiced in North Carolina, where future Supreme Court Justice James Iredell replied that such a danger, if it existed, was the price of liberty. He asked ". . . how is it possible to exclude any sect of men, without taking away the principle of religious freedom which we ourselves so warmly contend for? This is the foundation on which persecution has been raised in every part of the world. If you admit the least difference, the door to persecution is opened." Elliott, *Debates*, IV, 194.

38. Jefferson, *Works*, Ford ed., V, 80.

39. It is interesting to note that Madison narrowly avoided failing to be in a position to fulfill this promise. He failed of election to the first Senate and was opposed when he ran for the House of Representatives by a popular Baptist minister in a solidly Baptist district. The Baptists had opposed the adoption of the Constitution because it did not guarantee religious liberty. But they withdrew their opposition, such was their faith in Madison's word. The minister dropped out of the campaign and Madison was elected. See Wesley M. Gewehr, *The Great Awakening in Virginia, 1740-1790* (Durham, N. C., 1930), p. 189.

40. *Annals of Congress*, I, June 8, 1789, 434-435.

41. *Ibid.*, p. 755. Madison regretted deeply the fact that the amendment did not apply to states; he said, "If there were any reason to restrain the Government of the United States . . . it was equally necessary that they should be secured against the State Governments."

42. *Writings of Madison*, III, 275; ". . . the only effectual guard must be found in the soundness and stability of the general opinion on the subject."

43. *Ibid.*, I, 494 f.

44. Quoted in Mecklin, *The Story of American Dissent* (New York, 1934), p. 323.

45. Jefferson, *Writings*, Washington ed., VIII, 113.

46. *Ibid.*, V, 236. See to the same effect *Writings of Madison*, III, 273. Note also that Williams had expressed the same view over 150 years earlier; see *Bloudy Tenent of Persecution*, ed. E. B. Underhill (London, 1848), p. 321.

47. Quoted in G. Adolph Koch, *Republican Religion* (New York, 1933), p. 17.

48. The foregoing discussion of deism is largely based on Ralph B. Perry, *Puritanism and Democracy* (New York, 1944), pp. 151-165; also see Carl L. Becker, *The Declaration of Independence* (New York, 1945), Chap. 2; and Richard J. Purcell, *Connecticut in Transition, 1775-1818* (Washington, 1918), p. 39.

49. Sweet, pp. 334-336; Conrad H. Moehlman, *The Wall of Separation between Church and State* (Boston, 1951), pp. 100-101.

50. Jefferson, "Anas," *Works*, Ford ed., I, 284. Washington's Farewell Address contains such a reference to Christianity which was probably inspired, if not written, by Hamilton; see Wilfrid Parsons, *The First Freedom* (New York, 1948), p. 57. For more light on Washington's religious views see Charles A. Beard, *The Republic* (New York, 1943), pp. 169 f.; and Luigi Luzzatti, *God in Freedom*, trans. Alfonso Arbib-Costa, Supplementary Chapter by Max J. Kohler, (New York, 1930), pp. 695 ff.

51. Evarts B. Greene, *Religion and the State* (New York, 1941), p. 91. See also Jacob C. Meyer, *Church and State in Massachusetts from 1740 to 1833* (Cleveland, 1930), pp. 185 ff. Partly through the influence of Daniel Webster and Joseph Story this proposal was defeated. Adams's religious views are given in his letters to Jefferson.

52. Letter to Jefferson in Jefferson, *Writings*, Washington ed., VII, 396.

53. *Treaties and other International Acts of the United States of America* (Washington, 1931), II, 363-366. In 1815 after the Protestant revival the treaty was re-negotiated and the first of the two clauses was omitted.

54. The "Christian nation" argument is very common, especially among the more conservative religious groups—Catholics, Episcopalians, Lutherans, etc. For expositions of various degrees of the belief see Philip Schaff, *Church and State in the United States* ("Papers of the American Historical Association," Vol. II, No. 4 [1888]); Stephen Colwell, *The Position of Christianity in the United States* (Philadelphia, 1854); Wilfred Parsons, *The First Freedom;* R. Kemp Morton, *God in the Constitution* (Nashville, 1933); Isaac A. Cornelison, *The Relation of Religion to Civil Government in the United States of America*

(New York, 1895). In the hands of Catholic writers the argument seems self-defeating, for if we concede that this was a Christian nation in 1790, we must also concede, in view of the small minority of Catholics and the extreme fear of and hostility toward them, that it was also a Protestant nation; and that therefore if Christianity was established by the Constitution, it was *Protestant* Christianity.

55. Williams, "Letter to the Town of Providence" in F. W. Coker, *Democracy, Liberty and Property* (New York, 1949), pp. 305-306.

CHAPTER 4

1. Even Catholic liberal thinkers sometimes espouse this point of view; see, for example, Father J. Courtney Murray as quoted in Paul Hutchinson, *The New Leviathan* (Chicago, 1946), pp. 143 f.

2. Quoted in Sherman M. Smith, *The Relation of the State to Religious Education in Massachusetts* (Syracuse, N. Y., 1926), p. 28.

3. *Ibid.*, p. 15.   4. *Ibid.*, p. 44.

5. Thomas J. Wertenbaker, *The First Americans, 1607-1690* (New York, 1927), p. 140.

6. Slaughterhouse cases, 16 Wallace 36 (1873).

7. Reynolds v. United States, 98 U.S. 145 (1878); and cf. Davis v. Beason, 133 U.S. 333 (1890).

8. This fact was explicitly recognized as regards blasphemy by the Delaware court in an interesting opinion in Delaware v. Chandler, 2 Harr. 553, 573 (1837).

9. Church of the Holy Trinity v. United States, 143 U.S. 457, 470, 471, 472 (1892).

10. Donahoe v. Richards, 38 Maine 379, 409-410 (1854).

11. *Ibid.*, p. 410.

12. Nebraska v. Scheve, 93 Northwestern 169 (1903).

13. *Ibid.*, p. 170.

14. Those interested may see, as a starter, Moore v. Monroe, 64 Iowa 367; Spiller v. Woburn, 12 Allen (Mass.) 127; Wilkerson v. Rome, 152 Ga. 762; Church v. Bullock, 104 Texas 1; Evans v. Selma Union High School, 193 Calif. 54.

15. This is an evasion of the constitutional question of Sabbath legislation which is generally practiced in this country. See, for instance, Minnesota v. Petit, 74 Minn. 376, 177 U.S. 164.

16. Bloom v. Richards, 2 Ohio St. Rep. 387 (1853).

17. Board of Education v. Minor, 23 Ohio St. Rep. 211, 245, 246-251 (1872).

18. Wisconsin v. Weiss, 44 Northwestern 967, 975 (1890).

19. *Ibid.*, p. 981.

20. Herold v. Parish Board, 68 Southern 116, 121 (1915).

21. See, for instance, People *ex rel* Ring v. Board of Education, 245 Ill. 334; Synod of Dakota v. South Dakota, 50 Northwestern 632; Knowlton v. Baumhover, 182 Iowa 691; Perry v. Virginia, 44 Va. Rep. Ann. 809; Ayres v. Trustees of Methodist Episcopal Church, 3 Sandford 351 (Superior Court, N. Y.); Hale v. Everett, 53 New Hamp. 9.

22. Hamilton v. Regents of the University of California, 293 U.S. 245 (1934); Meyer v. Nebraska, 262 U.S. 390 (1923).

23. Cantwell v. Connecticut, 310 U.S. 296 (1940).

24. Everson v. Board of Education, 330 U.S. 1 (1947); People *ex rel* McCollum v. Board of Education, 333 U.S. 203 (1948).

25. Edward S. Corwin, "The Supreme Court as National School Board," *Thought*, XXIII (December, 1948), 665.

26. See Saia v. New York, 334 U.S. 558 (1948).

27. McCollum case, p. 238 (concurring opinion by Justice Jackson).

28. Clyde Summers. "The Sources and Limits of Religious Freedom," *Illinois Law Review*, XL (1946), 57. The analysis of the historical method here presented is largely taken from this excellent article.

29. Minersville School District v. Gobitis, 310 U.S. 586, 599 (1940).

30. West Virginia Board of Education v. Barnette, 319 U.S. 624 (1943).

31. *Ibid.*, p. 653 (dissenting opinion by Justice Frankfurter).

32. Frankfurter had feared that government's freedom of action would be unduly restricted if the Court were to strike down "reasonable" legislation. In his Barnette dissent he called such court action "a denial of the exercise of legislation." *Ibid.*, p. 654.

33. Gobitis case, pp. 602, 606 (dissenting opinion by Justice Stone).

34. Prince v. Massachusetts, 321 U.S. 158, 173-176 (1944) (dissenting opinion by Justice Murphy).

35. See, for instance, Kunz v. New York, 340 U.S. 290 (1951); Niemotko v. Maryland, 340 U.S. 268 (1951); Martin v. Struthers, 319 U.S. 141 (1943); Murdock v. Pennsylvania, 319 U.S. 105 (1943).

36. Alexander Meiklejohn, *Freedom and Its Relation to Self-Government* (New York, 1948).

37. Gobitis case, syllabus and pp. 594-595.

38. Jacobson v. Massachusetts, 197 U.S. 11 (1905).

39. Jones v. Opelika, 316 U.S. 584 (1942), reversed on rehearing, 319 U.S. 103 (1943); see also Prince v. Massachusetts.

40. Everson case, p. 28 (dissenting opinion by Justice Frankfurter).

41. Prince v. Massachusetts, p. 177 (dissenting opinion by Justice Jackson). See also Justice Jackson's concurring opinion in Douglas v. Jeannette, 319 U.S. 157, 166 (1943).

42. Corwin, p. 680.

43. Wilfrid Parsons, *The First Freedom* (New York, 1948), p. 178.

44. The significance of the later case of Zorach v. Clauson, 343 U.S. 306 (1952), which upheld New York City's "dismissed-time" program, is difficult to estimate. It is probable that it does not affect the argument here used, since the majority apparently assumed that no coercion was involved in New York's system.

45. Prince case, p. 174 (dissenting opinion by Justice Murphy).

46. It seems to be present implicitly, or even unconsciously, in Reynolds v. United States; Davis v. Beason; Taylor v. Mississippi, 319 U.S. 583 (1943); Martin v. Struthers; West Virginia v. Barnette; Cox v. New Hampshire, 312 U.S. 569 (1940); Jacobson v. Massachusetts.

47. Chief Justice Hughes for the majority in Cox v. New Hampshire.

48. Summers, p. 73.

49. See also Chaplinsky v. New Hampshire, 315 U.S. 568 (1942), in which Murphy himself upheld the state's dignity against the religious freedom to curse its officials!

50. Jacobson v. Massachusetts.   51. Cantwell v. Connecticut.

52. McCollum case, p. 213 (concurring opinion by Justice Frankfurter).

53. Everson case, p. 15 (majority opinion by Justice Black).

54. The fact that America is primarily Christian, and rather orthodoxly so, may also make the Court particularly conscious of the rights of small minorities with unorthodox beliefs and practices and of their need for special protection.

55. Another grave and extremely interesting problem which has confronted the courts is the question of how much credence is to be given to the protestations of sincerity made by practitioners of strange and unusual religious beliefs,

such as, perhaps, snake worship or snake tests. The Supreme Court met this problem head on in United States v. Ballard, 322 U.S. 78 (1944), which involved a case of what the Court felt was the old confidence game in a new guise, prac-·· ticed by the leader of the "I AM" cult. The majority was inclined for obvious reasons to evade the issue of the sincerity of the defendant's religious beliefs. Justice Jackson wrote a particularly perspicacious dissent ·maintaining that a man's beliefs cannot be called insincere merely because they differ from the prevailing ones. A court, said he, was in no position to judge the truth or falsity of any religious belief; obviously it could not, therefore, pin the label of insincerity on a belief which could not be proved false.

CHAPTER 5

1. Pierce v. Society of the Sisters of the Holy Name, 268 U.S. 510 (1925).
2. See Pope Pius XI, "Encyclical Letter on the Christian Education of Youth," reprinted in *Current History*, XXXI (March, 1930), 1091.
3. Evidence to this effect are the many writings by church leaders on the subject. The following are illustrative: Pius XI, *op. cit.*; George U. Wenner, *Religious Education and the Public School* (Philadelphia, 1920), pp. 26 ff; Sister Mary of St. Michael Hubner, *Professional Attitudes Toward Religion in the Public Schools* . . . (Washington, 1944), p. 21; Paul Hutchinson, *The New Leviathan* (Chicago, 1946), pp. 195, 198 f.; Winthrop Hudson, *The Great Tradition of the American Churches* (New York, 1953), pp. 17, 21, *et passim*; Conrad H. Moehlman, *The Wall of Separation Between Church and State* (Boston, 1951), pp. 155-156.
4. See, for expressions of this point of view, Hubner, p. 8; Wenner; Pius XI; and Samuel M. Cavert, "Points of Tension Between Church and State in America Today," in Henry P. Van Dusen *et al.*, *Church and State in the Modern World* (New York, 1937), p. 167.
5. Justice Jackson for the majority in Wickard v. Fillburn, 317 U.S. 111 (1942).
6. Such a viewpoint may be found in T. W. M. Marshall, "Secular Education in England and the United States," *American Catholic Quarterly Review*, I (1876); F. Ernest Johnson, "Religion and the Philosophy of Education," *Vital Speeches*, VII (November 1, 1940), 40; Walter S. Athearn, *Religious Education and American Democracy* (Boston, 1917); Wilfrid Parsons, *The First Freedom* (New York, 1948), p. 108. Some writers have tried to refute such arguments; see V. T. Thayer, *Religion in Public Education* (New York, 1947), pp. 99 ff; Sidney Hook, "The New Failure of Nerve," *Partisan Review*, X (January-February, 1943), 2.
7. For expositions of this point of view see Parsons, p. 178; and Edward S. Corwin, "The Supreme Court as National School Board," *Thought*, XXIII (December, 1948), 680 ff. This is a typical Catholic definition of liberty.
8. Alvin W. Johnson and Frank H. Yost, *Separation of Church and State in the United States* (Minneapolis, 1948), pp. 41-73.
9. See Frank H. Knight, "Theology and Education," *American Journal of Sociology*, XLIV (March, 1939), p. 658.
10. Marshall, p. 288.   11. Hudson, p. 249.
12. Such programs have been widely discussed. See Johnson and Yost, pp. 74-90, for some description of them.
13. McCollum and Zorach cases, cited in Chap. 4, notes 24 and 44.
14. See Johnson and Yost, pp. 91-131. 15. *Ibid.*, p. 114.
16. See *ibid.*, pp. 146-164.
17. Everson case, cited in Chap. 4, note 24.

18. See John M. Mecklin, *The Story of American Dissent* (New York, 1934) for a full sociological analysis of this process.

19. Gobitis and Barnette cases, cited in Chap. 4, notes 29 and 30; and see Johnson and Yost, pp. 175-198.   20. See Johnson and Yost, pp. 219-255.

21. See Cavert, pp. 169-174; Hutchinson, pp. 228 f.

22. See Hutchinson, Chap. 3.   23. Cavert, p. 176.

24. Cavert, p. 177; see also Hutchinson, pp. 63 f.   25. See Hutchinson, p. 64.

CHAPTER 6

1. For a trenchant application of this idea to a different field see Robert S. Platt, "Environmentalism versus Geography," *American Journal of Sociology*, LIII (March, 1948), 351-358. A similar idea is expressed in Hans J. Morgenthau, "The Limitations of Science and the Problems of Social Planning," *Social Science 200—Selected Readings* (University of Chicago, 1949), p. 30.

2. Robert M. Johnston, *The Roman Theocracy and the Republic, 1846-1849* (London, 1901), p. 24. On p. 6 Johnston refers to "the theocratical government of Rome" as "nearly constantly a feeble misrule of the worst character." He also (pp. 19-28) gives a brief description of the governmental institutions of the declining Papal States; his description is not necessarily true of their earlier history. Cf. Arthur N. Holcombe, *The Foundations of the Modern Commonwealth* (New York, 1923), p. 102.

3. See Robert I. Calhoun, "Church, State, and Human Devotion," in Henry P. Van Dusen *et al., Church and State in the Modern World* (New York, 1937), p. 47. Cf. John M. Mecklin, *The Story of American Dissent* (New York, 1934), p. 103.

4. John Locke, *A Letter Concerning Toleration*, ed. Charles L. Sherman (New York, 1937), p. 220; cf. p. 184.

5. Roger Williams, "Letter to the Town of Providence," in F. W. Coker, *Democracy, Liberty and Property* (New York, 1949), pp. 305-306.

6. Thomas Jefferson, *Writings*, Washington ed., VIII, 113.

7. *Records of Rhode Island*, II, 1; and see quotation *supra*, p. 54.

8. Locke, pp. 198-199.   9. Jefferson, VIII, 113.

10. See, for instance, Otto Gierke, *Political Theories of the Middle Age*, trans. Frederic W. Maitland (Cambridge, 1900), pp. 10-12.

11. See Church of the Holy Trinity v. United States, 143 U.S. 457 (1891), for an example.

12. See Robert S. and Helen M. Lynd, *Middletown* (New York, 1929), pp. 317, 493 f.; and *Middletown in Transition* (New York, 1937), p. 462.

13. See Albert C. Dieffenbach, *Religious Liberty, the Great American Illusion* (New York, 1927), pp. 138-142; Mecklin, *op. cit.*, pp. 348-355; Harold J. Laski, *The American Democracy* (New York, 1948), p. 295.

14. See John N. Figgis, *Churches in the Modern State* (London, 1913), pp. 14 f., 43 f.

15. See, for arguments to this effect, Sidney Hook, "The New Failure of Nerve," *Partisan Review*, X (January-February, 1943), 2 ff.; Horace M. Kallen, "Churchmen's Claims on the Public School," *The Nation's Schools*, XXIX (May, 1942), 50; V. T. Thayer, *Religion in Public Education* (New York, 1947), pp. 105-113; Harold J. Laski, *op. cit.*, p. 313.

16. For the concept of totalitarian democracy see J. L. Talmon, *The Rise of Totalitarian Democracy* (Boston, 1952), pp. 1-13.

17. See Heinrich A. Rommen, *The State in Catholic Thought* (St. Louis, 1945), for an exhaustive discussion of Catholic theories of the state.

CHAPTER 7

1. The same can be said for the statesman.
2. For instance, Carl J. Friedrich, *The New Belief in the Common Man* (Boston, 1942), pp. 43-59, 79.
3. See A. D. Lindsay, *The Modern Democratic State* (New York, 1947), p. 27.
4. R. M. MacIver, *Leviathan and the People* (University, La., 1939), pp. 29, 72.
5. MacIver, *The Web of Government* (New York, 1947), pp. 410 ff.
6. Since this analysis is particularly concerned with the United States, the author sees no point in considering whether or not MacIver's multi-group theory is universally valid.
7. Friedrich, p. 153; but cf. Heinrich A. Rommen, *The State in Catholic Thought* (St. Louis, 1945), pp. 276 ff. for a somewhat contrary view.
8. Voluntary in the sense that there is no compulsion to belong to any particular sect or espouse any particular belief; one is not born into a church in the same sense as one is born into a state, and the church can expel a member as punishment, which the modern state cannot generally do.
9. Aristotle, *Politics*, trans. and ed. Ernest Barker (Oxford, 1946), pp. 40 ff.
10. Rommen, p. 280; and see MacIver, *Web of Government*, pp. 182-184; Friedrich, p. 161; Lindsay, p. 265.
11. *Supra*, p. 126.
12. This subject is discussed in some detail from the sociological and anthropological points of view in Joachim Wach, *Sociology of Religion* (Chicago, 1944), pp. 27-34; and see the numerous references therein cited.
13. Francesco Ruffini, *Religious Liberty*, trans. J. Parker Heyes (New York, 1912), pp. 511-514; and see Albert C. Dieffenbach, *Religious Liberty, the Great American Illusion* (New York, 1927), *passim.*
14. Because morals cannot be invoked to settle issues involving a dispute as to what the morals should be. Political action in a democracy therefore consists in creating "from contradictory claims an ideal that will satisfy both, or at least not leave either dissatisfied enough to prefer insurrection to acquiescence." This means, however, that the basic issues which cannot be compromised must be left strictly alone by politicians, which is what the First Amendment seeks to ensure and what the author is trying to prove desirable. See T. V. Smith, *The Legislative Way of Life* (Chicago, 1940), p. 28 and *passim.*
15. See Lindsay, p. 60.
16. As a corollary the state becomes incapable of deciding what is religious truth, since both the many religious associations existing within its jurisdiction and the number of individuals not belonging to any of them have the right to believe as they in conscience desire. Theoretically, truth in religion becomes, for the state, what each citizen or church believes it to be. This is bulwarked by the fact that religious truth, however true it may be, is not susceptible of proof in the ordinary manner. A scientific truth may be proved in such a manner that continued disbelief only makes one ridiculous; but theological truth may be disbelieved without such an effect. In fact, an attempt to prove it is merely likely to stir up an attempt to disprove it which may be just as convincing theologically as the original proof. This is a characteristic also shared by philosophy. The controversy over whether or not the world is round has been settled because the proofs convinced everyone; but the dispute over the Trinity has not, because the truth or falsity cannot be empirically proved. This does not mean that the Trinity is not as true as the sphericity of the earth, but only that its truth cannot be proved in a way that will convince him who does not wish to be convinced. See J. B. Bury, *History of Freedom of Thought* (New

York, 1913), p. 17; A. N. Holcombe, *Foundations of the Modern Commonwealth* (New York, 1923), pp. 117-125. Also note Justice Jackson's discerning dissent in United States v. Ballard, 332 U.S. 78 (1944).

17. See Lindsay, p. 209. This is a restatement of St. Optatus's fourth-century view that the church is in the state rather than vice versa. Cf. C. H. McIlwain, *Growth of Political Thought in the West* (New York, 1932), p. 164.

18. The Catholic church accepts separation as an expedient in such circumstances; Rommen, pp. 600, 603-605. But I reject Rommen's contention that separation is merely a political expedient rather than a philosophical principle. My view is that the state is, as shown above, intrinsically incapable of judging religious truth; the religious equality implied in the separation principle is thus necessary not because all religions are actually equal but because the state is no fit judge. In support of Rommen's statement of Catholic principle see two other Catholic writers, Wilfrid Parsons, *The First Freedom* (New York, 1948), p. 103 f.; and Jacques Maritain, *The Rights of Man and Natural Law,* trans. Doris Anson (New York, 1943), p. 26 f.

19. See Rommen, p. 571.

20. Rommen, p. 579; cf. Pope Pius XI, "Encyclical Letter on the Christian Education of Youth," *Current History,* XXXI (March, 1930), 1093.

21. Even though the church be regarded as divine, it cannot be accepted that the mantle of divinity extends to the individuals who compose it. To the state it must ever remain an institution composed of fallible human beings. Thus even though a citizen may subject himself ecclesiastically to a church, he cannot in conscience do so politically; particularly, as Figgis points out, because in so doing he would be acting for the good of a particular group rather than for the common good. See John N. Figgis, *Churches in the Modern State* (London, 1913), pp. 113-135; cf. Maritain, pp. 26 f.

22. See Sidney Hook, "The New Failure of Nerve," *Partisan Review,* X (January-February, 1943), 23; as Paul Hutchinson says, "the relativity which we try to get rid of when we proclaim the authority of the moral law slips in the back door again when we turn to the task of applying it." *The New Leviathan* (Chicago, 1946), p. 167, and see p. 181.

23. For example, Wilbur G. Katz, "Freedom of Religion and State Neutrality," *University of Chicago Law Review,* XX (Spring, 1953), 426-440.

24. See Holcombe, p. 287.

25. Luigi Sturzo, *Church and State* (New York, 1939), p. 547; Hutchinson, pp. 183 ff.

26. S. M. Cavert, "Points of Tension Between Church and State in America Today," in H. P. Van Dusen *et al., Church and State in the Modern World* (New York, 1937), p. 182.

27. Figgis, p. 113.   28. Figgis, p. 130; cf Hutchinson, pp. 185 ff.

29. W. S. Hudson, *The Great Tradition of the American Churches* (New York, 1953), Foreword and pp. 243-263.

30. Friedrich, p. 153.

31. See J. M. Mecklin, *The Story of American Dissent* (New York, 1934), pp. 341-371, for a spirited indictment of the Protestant churches on this count; and the Lynds' Middletown studies for a sociological study, especially *Middletown in Transition* (New York, 1937), pp. 295-318. And see the recent criticism of the churches in W. S. Hudson, *op cit.*

32. See Hutchinson, pp. 68 ff.   33. See Lindsay, p. 210.

34. Ralph B. Perry, *Puritanism and Democracy* (New York, 1944), p. 349.

A Selected Bibliography

ADAMS, Brooks. *The Emancipation of Massachusetts.* Boston: Houghton Mifflin Co., 1893.

ADAMS, Charles Francis. *Three Episodes of Massachusetts History,* rev. ed. 2 vols. Boston: Houghton Mifflin Co., 1903.

ADAMS, Herbert B. *The Church and Popular Education.* Baltimore: Johns Hopkins Press, 1900.

ADAMS, James Truslow. *The History of New England,* Vol. I, *The Founding of New England.* Boston: Little, Brown & Co., 1921.

————. *Provincial Society, 1690-1763. (A History of American Life,* ed. A. M. Schlesinger and D. R. Fox, Vol. III.) New York: Macmillan Co., 1927.

ALLEN, John W. *English Political Thought, 1603-1660,* Vol. I. London: Methuen & Co., 1938.

AMBLER, Charles Henry. *Sectionalism in Virginia from 1776 to 1861.* Chicago: University of Chicago Press, 1910.

APPLEGARTH, Albert C. *Quakers in Pennsylvania.* Baltimore: Johns Hopkins Press, 1892.

ATHEARN, Walter Scott. *Religious Education and American Democracy.* Boston: Pilgrim Press, 1917.

BARBER, Hollis W. "Religious Liberty v. Police Power: Jehovah's Witnesses," *American Political Science Review,* XLI (April, 1947), 226-247.

BARKER, Arthur. *Milton and the Puritan Dilemma, 1641-1660.* Toronto: University of Toronto Press, 1942.

BELASCO, Philip S. *Authority in Church and State.* London: George Allen & Unwin, 1928.

BELL, Sadie. *The Church, the State, and Education in Virginia.* Philadelphia: Science Press, 1930.

BOAS, Ralph and Louise. *Cotton Mather, Keeper of the Puritan Conscience.* New York: Harper & Bros., 1928.

BRADY, Joseph H. *Confusion Twice Confounded: the First Amendment and the Supreme Court.* South Orange, N. J.: Seton Hall University Press, 1955.

BROWN, Samuel Windsor. *The Secularization of American Education.* New York: Teachers College, Columbia University, 1912.

BURY, John B. *A History of Freedom of Thought.* New York: Henry Holt & Co., 1913.

COBB, Sanford H. *The Rise of Religious Liberty in America.* New York: Macmillan Co., 1902.

COLWELL, Stephen. *The Position of Christianity in the United States.* Philadelphia: Lippincott, Grambo, 1854.

COONS, Paul Wakeman. *The Achievement of Religious Liberty in Connecticut.* New Haven: Yale University Press, 1936.

CORNELISON, Isaac A. *The Relation of Religion to Civil Government in the United State of America.* New York: G. P. Putnam's Sons, 1895.

CORWIN, Edward S. "The Supreme Court as National School Board," *Thought,* XXIII (December, 1948), 665.

CREIGHTON, Mandell. *Persecution and Tolerance.* London: Longmans, Green & Co., 1895.

CROOKER, Joseph Henry. *The Winning of Religious Liberty.* Boston: Pilgrim Press, 1918.

DAWSON, Christopher. *Religion and the Modern State.* New York: Sheed & Ward, 1936.

DIEFFENBACH, Albert C. *Religious Liberty, the Great American Illusion.* New York: William Morrow & Co., 1927.

ECKENRODE, H. J. *Separation of Church and State in Virginia.* Richmond: Virginia State Library, 1909.

ELLIS, George E. *The Puritan Age and Rule in the Colony of Massachusetts Bay, (1629-1685).* Boston: Houghton, Mifflin Co., 1888.

ERNST, James E. *The Political Thought of Roger Williams.* Seattle: University of Washington Press, 1929.

FIGGIS, John Neville. *Churches in the Modern State.* London: Longmans, Green & Co., 1913.

FRIEDRICH, Carl J. *The New Belief in the Common Man.* Boston: Beacon Press, 1942.

GAVIN, Frank. *Seven Centuries of the Problem of Church and State.* Princeton: Princeton University Press, 1938.

GEWEHR, Wesley M. *The Great Awakening in Virginia, 1740-1790.* Durham, N. C.: Duke University Press, 1930.

GOBBEL, Luther L. *Church-State Relationships in Education in North Carolina since 1776.* Durham, N. C.: Duke University Press, 1938.

GOOCH, George P. *English Democratic Ideas in the Seventeenth Century.* Cambridge: Cambridge University Press, 1927.

GOSLIN, Ryllis Alexander. *Church and State.* New York: Foreign Policy Association, 1937.

GREENE, Evarts B. "Persistent Problems of Church and State," *American Historical Review,* XXXVI (January, 1931), 257-273.

————. *Religion and the State: the Making and Testing of an American Tradition.* New York: New York University Press, 1941.

GREENE, M. Louise. *The Development of Religious Liberty in Connecticut.* Boston: Houghton, Mifflin Co., 1905.

GWATKIN, Henry Melville. *Church and State in England to the Death of Queen Anne.* London: Longmans, Green & Co., 1917.

HAAS, John A. W. *The Problem of the Christian State.* Boston: Stratford, 1928.

HANUS, Paul H. "School Instruction in Religion," *Education,* XXVII (September, 1906), 10-17, and (October, 1906), 73-84.

HARRINGTON, James. *The Oceana of James Harrington, and his other Works: . . . ,* ed. John Toland. London, 1700.

HARTNETT, Robert C. *Equal Rights for Children.* New York: America Press, n.d.

HOBBES, Thomas. *The Elements of Law, Natural and Politic,* ed. Ferdinand Tonnies. Cambridge: Cambridge University Press, 1928.

BIBLIOGRAPHY

HOBBES, Thomas. *The English Works of Thomas Hobbes of Malmesbury,* ed. William Molesworth. 11 vols. London: John Bohn, 1839-1845.

HOLCOMBE, A. N. *Foundations of the Modern Commonwealth.* New York: Harper & Bros., 1923.

HOOK, Sidney. "The New Failure of Nerve," *Partisan Review,* X (January-February, 1943), 2-23.

HUBNER, Sister Mary of St. Michael. *Professional Attitudes Toward Religion in the Public Schools of the United States Since 1900.* Washington: Catholic University of America Press, 1944.

HUDSON, Winthrop S. *The Great Tradition of the American Churches.* New York: Harper & Bros., 1953.

HUTCHINSON, Paul. *The New Leviathan.* Chicago: Willett, Clark, 1946.

JAMES, Charles F. *Documentary History of the Struggle for Religious Liberty in Virginia.* Lynchburg, Va., J. P. Bell, 1900.

JEFFERSON, Thomas. *The Commonplace Book,* ed. Gilbert Chinard. Baltimore: Johns Hopkins Press, 1926.

————. *Writings,* ed. H. A. Washington. 9 vols. New York: John O. Riker, 1853-1854.

JOHNSON, Alvin W., and YOST, Frank H. *Separation of Church and State in the United States.* Minneapolis: University of Minnesota Press, 1948.

JOHNSON, F. Ernest. "Religion and the Philosophy of Education," *Vital Speeches,* VII (November 1, 1940), 35-39.

JORDAN, Wilbur K. *The Development of Religious Toleration in England.* Vols. I, II. London: George Allen & Unwin, 1932, 1936. Vols. III, IV. Cambridge, Mass.: Harvard University Press, 1938, 1940.

KATZ, Wilber G. "Freedom of Religion and State Neutrality," *University of Chicago Law Review,* XX (Spring, 1953), 426-440.

KNIGHT, Frank H. "Theology and Education," *American Journal of Sociology,* XLIV (March, 1939), 649-679.

KOCH, G. Adolph. *Republican Religion.* New York: Henry Holt & Co., 1933.

LAUER, Paul E. *Church and State in New England.* Baltimore: Johns Hopkins Press, 1892.

LINDSAY, A. D. *The Modern Democratic State.* New York: Oxford University Press, 1947.

LOCKE, John. *A Letter Concerning Toleration,* ed. Charles L. Sherman. New York: Appleton-Century Co., 1937.

LUZZATTI, Luigi. *God in Freedom.* Translated by Alfonso Arbib-Costa, with a supplementary chapter by Max J. Kohler. New York: Macmillan, 1930.

LYON, Thomas. *The Theory of Religious Liberty in England, 1603-1639.* Cambridge: Cambridge University Press, 1937.

MCILWAINE, Henry R. *The Struggle of Protestant Dissenters for Religious Toleration in Virginia.* Baltimore: Johns Hopkins Press, 1894.

MACIVER, Robert M. *Leviathan and the People.* University, La.: Louisiana State University Press, 1939.

————. *The Web of Government.* New York: Macmillan Co., 1947.

MADISON, James. *Letters and other Writings.* Library of Congress Edition. 4 vols. Philadelphia: J. B. Lippincott & Co., 1865.

MARITAIN, Jacques. *The Rights of Man and Natural Law.* Translated by Doris C. Anson. New York: Charles Scribner's Sons, 1943.

MECKLIN, John M. *The Story of American Dissent.* New York: Harcourt, Brace & Co., 1934.

173

MEYER, Jacob C. *Church and State in Massachusetts from 1740 to 1833.* Cleveland: Western Reserve University Press, 1930.

MILLER, Perry. *The New England Mind: the Seventeenth Century.* New York: Macmillan Co., 1939.

——————. *Orthodoxy in Massachusetts, 1630-1650; a Genetic Study.* Cambridge, Mass.: Harvard University Press, 1933.

——————. *Roger Williams: His Contribution to the American Tradition.* Indianapolis: Bobbs-Merrill Co., 1953.

MILTON, John. *The Prose Works of John Milton,* ed. J. A. St. John. 5 vols. London: George Bell & Sons, 1909.

MOEHLMAN, Conrad H. *The Wall of Separation between Church and State.* Boston: Beacon Press, 1951.

MORAIS, Herbert H. *Deism in Eighteenth Century America.* New York: Columbia University Press, 1934.

MORTON, R. Kemp. *God in the Constitution.* Nashville: Cokesbury Press, 1933.

O'NEILL, J. M. *Religion and Education under the Constitution.* New York: Harper & Bros., 1949.

PARKES, Henry Bamford. "John Cotton and Roger Williams Debate Toleration, 1644-1652," *New England Quarterly,* IV (October, 1931), 735-756.

PARRINGTON, Vernon Louis. *Main Currents in American Thought,* Vol. I, *The Colonial Mind.* New York: Harcourt, Brace & Co., 1927.

PARSONS, Wilfrid. *The First Freedom.* New York: Declan X. McMullen, 1948.

PENN, William. *A Collection of the Works of William Penn.* 2 vols. London, 1726.

PERRY, Ralph Barton. *Puritanism and Democracy.* New York: Vanguard Press, 1944.

PETRIE, George. *Church and State in Early Maryland.* Baltimore: Johns Hopkins Press, 1892.

PFEFFER, Leo. *Church, State and Freedom.* Boston: Beacon Press, 1953.

PIUS XI. "Encyclical Letter on the Christian Education of Youth," *Current History,* XXXI (March, 1930), 1091-1104.

POST, Truman R. *The Skeptical Era in Modern History.* New York: C. Scribner, 1856.

PURCELL, Richard J. *Connecticut in Transition, 1775-1818.* Washington: American Historical Association, 1918.

REED, Susan Martha. *Church and State in Massachusetts, 1691-1740.* Urbana: University of Illinois Press, 1914.

ROBINSON, William A. *Jeffersonian Democracy in New England.* New Haven: Yale University Press, 1916.

ROMMEN, Heinrich A. *The State in Catholic Thought.* St. Louis: B. Herder, 1945.

RUFFINI, Francesco. *Religious Liberty.* Translated by J. Parker Heyes. New York: G. P. Putnam's Sons, 1912.

RUSSELL SMITH, Hugh F. *Harrington and his Oceana.* Cambridge: Cambridge University Press, 1914.

——————. *The Theory of Religious Liberty in the Reigns of Charles II and James II.* Cambridge: Cambridge University Press, 1911.

SCHAFF, Philip. *The Progress of Religious Freedom.* New York: Charles Scribner's Sons, 1889.

SCHNEIDER, Herbert W. *The Puritan Mind.* New York: Henry Holt & Co., 1930.

SCOTT, Nancy E. *The Limits of Toleration within the Church of England from 1632 to 1642.* Philadelphia [Lancaster, Pa., The New Era Printing Co.] 1912.

BIBLIOGRAPHY

SEATON, A. A. *The Theory of Toleration under the Later Stuarts.* Cambridge: Cambridge University Press, 1911.

SMITH, Sherman M. *The Relation of the State to Religious Education in Massachusetts.* Syracuse: Syracuse University Bookstore, 1926.

STOKES, Anson Phelps. *Church and State in the United States.* 3 vols. New York: Harper & Bros., 1950.

STRAUS, Oscar S. *Religious Liberty in the United States.* New York: Philip Cowen, 1896.

STRICKLAND, Reba C. *Religion and the State in Georgia in the Eighteenth Century.* New York: Columbia University Press, 1939.

STURZO, Luigi. *Church and State.* New York: Longmans, Green & Co., 1939.

SUMMERS, Clyde W. "The Sources and Limits of Religious Freedom," *Illinois Law Review,* XLI (May-July, 1946), 53-80.

SWEET, William Warren. "Natural Religion and Religious Liberty in America," *Journal of Religion,* XXV (January, 1945), 45-55.

————. *Religion in Colonial America.* New York: Charles Scribner's Sons, 1942.

THAYER, V. T. *Religion in Public Education.* New York: Viking Press, 1947.

THOM, Willam Taylor. *The Struggle for Religious Freedom in Virginia: the Baptists.* Baltimore: Johns Hopkins Press, 1900.

THORNING, Joseph Francis. *Religious Liberty in Transition.* New York: Benziger Bros., 1931.

TORPEY, William G. *Judicial Doctrines of Religious Rights in America.* Chapel Hill: University of North Carolina Press, 1948.

VAN DUSEN, Henry P., *et al. Church and State in the Modern World.* New York: Harper & Bros., 1937.

WACH, Joachim. *Sociology of Religion.* Chicago: University of Chicago Press, 1944.

WEEKS, Stephen B. *The Religious Development in the Province of North Carolina.* Baltimore: Johns Hopkins Press, 1892.

————. *Church and State in North Carolina.* Baltimore: Johns Hopkins Press, 1893.

WENNER, George U. *Religious Education and the Public School.* Philadelphia: United Lutheran Publication House, 1920.

WERTENBAKER, Thomas Jefferson. *The First Americans, 1607-1690. (A History of American Life,* ed. A. M. Schlesinger and D. R. Fox, Vol. II) New York: Macmillan Co., 1927.

————. *The Founding of American Civilization: the Puritan Oligarchy.* New York: Charles Scribner's Sons, 1947.

WILLIAMS, Roger. *The Bloudy Tenent of Persecution for cause of Consciense Discussed.* ed. E. B. Underhill. London: Hanserd Knollys Society, 1848.

————. *The Bloody Tenent yet More Bloody; by Mr. Cottons endevour to wash it white in the Blood of the Lambe:* . . . London: 1652.

WOLFE, Don M. *Milton in the Puritan Revolution.* New York: Thomas Nelson & Sons, 1941.

ZOLLMANN, Carl. *American Church Law.* St. Paul: West Publishing Co., 1933.

175

Index